TOOLKIT FOR
Turbulence

TOOLKIT FOR
Turbulence

THE MINDSET AND METHODS
THAT LEADERS NEED TO
TURN ADVERSITY TO ADVANTAGE

Graham Winter
Martin Bean

WILEY

Do you want to turn the adversity of disruption into an opportunity to grow and to be a better leader?

Are you always thinking about how to equip, develop and support your team to be the best they can be?

Are performance <u>and</u> wellbeing important to you?

If you've answered yes to any of these questions, then you are an *advantage leader,* and we welcome you to our community!

You're about to read a book full of tools for leaders of every type and at all levels who are striving to turn the disruptions of technology, the economy, pandemics and social change into advantage. It's a *Toolkit for Turbulence*.

Just a few years ago the pace of change began to accelerate, driven by leaps in technology, shifts in cultural values and priorities, and the opportunities and threats of a connected world.

Then along came the pandemic, and what looked like a full stop on progress is now revealing itself as the fuel that *accelerated change* in the world of work.

Today, on the cusp of the AI revolution, we live in an age of disruption, of never-ending volatility, uncertainty, complexity and ambiguity.

Words like *fatigued*, *overwhelmed* and *uncertain* pepper workplace conversations, but there are leaders who see it differently.

Before, during and following the COVID-19 pandemic these leaders welcomed disruption, grasped the opportunities to adapt at pace, and built teams and cultures that are turning the adversity of disruption into the advantage of being adaptable and resilient. We call these people *advantage leaders*.

How do you view disruption? Can you imagine the possibilities if you and your team were to grow stronger when contending with disruption? Are you willing to accept that success is about transformation, and it starts with you? If yes, then let's go!

Thank you

A massive thank you to each of the following *advantage leaders* who so generously offered their time and wisdom to benefit other leaders. Please note that the positions outlined below are those at the time of interview for the book.

Andrew McConville, Chief Executive, Murray–Darling Basin Authority

Andrew Westacott, Chief Executive Officer, Australian Grand Prix Corporation

Anna Wenngren, Chief People Officer, SafetyCulture

Ashley Ross, Founder and Head Coach, Coach Learning Solutions

Bernadette McDonald, Chief Executive Officer, The Royal Children's Hospital Melbourne

Brett Wickham, Managing Director, ACCIONA Energía Australia

Chris Tanti, Chief Executive Officer, Leukaemia Foundation

Kate Koch, Chief Financial Officer, SEEK

Kevin Sullivan, Captain (retired) and author of *No Man's Land*

Paul Duldig, Chief Executive Officer, State Library Victoria

Paul Ostrowski, Chief Executive Officer, Care Connect

Rebecca James, Group Chief Executive Officer, **humm**group

Robert Iervasi, former Group Chief Executive Officer, Asahi Beverages Oceania Region

Sally Capp AO, Lord Mayor of Melbourne, City of Melbourne

Professor Tanya Monro AC, Chief Defence Scientist, Defence Science and Technology Group, Department of Defence

First published in 2024 by John Wiley & Sons Australia, Ltd
Level 4, 600 Bourke St, Melbourne, Victoria 3000, Australia

Typeset in Raleway Regular 11/15pt

© The Bean Centre Pty Ltd and World Competitive People Pty Ltd T/A
Think One Team Consulting 2024

The moral rights of the authors have been asserted

ISBN: 978-1-394-20865-4

A catalogue record for this
book is available from the
National Library of Australia

Cover design by Wiley
Cover Images: © Pixxsa / Adobe Stock

Disclaimer

The material in this publication is of the nature of general comment only, and does not represent professional advice. It is not intended to provide specific guidance for particular circumstances and it should not be relied on as the basis for any decision to take action or not take action on any matter which it covers. Readers should obtain professional advice where appropriate, before making any such decision. To the maximum extent permitted by law, the authors and publisher disclaim all responsibility and liability to any person, arising directly or indirectly from any person taking or not taking action based on the information in this publication.

Printed in Singapore
M125925_080923

From Graham Winter

To Carol, and to Mark, Kate, Leo and Eva, and Ben, Kim and Jackson

From Martin Bean

To Mary, and to Maddie, Georgie and Harriet

Contents

Introduction

This book will give you deep practical insights into the thinking, behaviours and tools of leaders who thrive in times of turbulence. You will hear about the fundamental mindsets that can make or break people and teams during disruption. You will learn how to recalibrate your thinking to suit a continually disrupted world. You will be introduced to frameworks to form, build and accelerate the performance and wellbeing of your team, and learn how to scale this approach across your life, team and enterprise.

This is not a theoretical or academic book, and neither is it a typical management or self-help guide. The ideas covered are drawn from the experiences of highly successful leaders who are navigating the emotional roller coaster of the pandemic and its aftermath. They have coached, cared for and built high-performing teams. They have rebounded from setbacks such as cyber-attacks, supply chain disruption and massive budget shortfalls, and pivoted then pivoted again when the unimaginable has become the inevitable.

Their mindset and leadership toolkit helped them to be the best leaders they could be and to coach others to unlock their potential at a time when the default response for many was to be more defensive and protective. If you are reading this book, our guess is you'd also like to bring your best self to leadership, when and where it is needed, and to unlock the potential of the people, teams and enterprises you lead. In short, you want to be an advantage leader.

Six parts

At every step in this book's development we have reminded ourselves that most leaders are time poor, yet they aspire to learn about and apply better and proven tools to bring out the best in themselves and their teams in a turbulent business environment. We applied three tests when choosing content to frame and fill the book:

> » **simple, easy-to-apply tools** to effect positive change in personal leadership and team behaviours

> » **pragmatic and expert guidance** from people who are practising these techniques on the 'front line' so readers can trust in the source and content

> » **proven working models** using performance psychology principles to change habits and enable quick, simple and effective implementation.

Toolkit for Turbulence is divided into six parts, each with a core theme and a brief description of the intent.

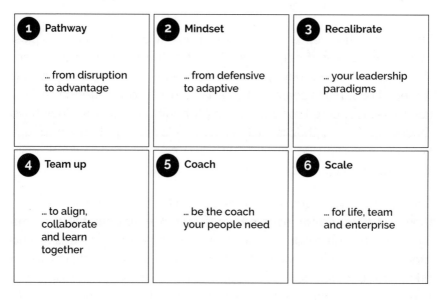

1 Pathway	**2** Mindset	**3** Recalibrate
... from disruption to advantage	... from defensive to adaptive	... your leadership paradigms
4 Team up	**5** Coach	**6** Scale
... to align, collaborate and learn together	... be the coach your people need	... for life, team and enterprise

The book is designed around a combination of real-life stories, working models and practical tools featuring contributions from top Australian and international business leaders. Visual canvases and step-by-step tool guides simplify the techniques, and (with additional online resources) make them quick and easy to apply.

Here is a quick guide to terminology, so you can see how it all fits together:

» **Tools**. These are practical resources designed to help you to address and overcome leadership challenges and unlock potential. Twenty-five *primary tools* are the 'go-to' guide to master key challenges, and these are supported by a host of *secondary tools* and activities to encourage reflection and stimulate insights.

» **Models**. Leaders encounter a great deal of complexity, and that's where models help to simplify complex concepts and pave the way to successfully implement tools and practices. You'll find engaging and thought-provoking models spread throughout the book along with examples to illustrate how leaders apply them to advantage.

» **Canvases**. A distinctive feature of *Toolkit for Turbulence* is the use of canvases as visual guides to organise thoughts and map action plans. These are incorporated into individual tools and are used to organise multiple tools. For example, the *Team Canvas* is a blueprint for setting up a high-performing team and draws on the outputs of a variety of team-building tools.

Building your own toolkit

In our consulting we are often asked the best way to construct a leadership toolkit and we always reply there is no one right way.

This book describes approaches that are proven to be effective across a wide variety of settings where uncertainty and complexity are rampant. Stories from the field will show you how to design and use tools for yourself, with your team and in the wider enterprise or ecosystem. You can follow the instructions or modify them to suit your preferences or circumstances.

Here are three options to consider based on ways that people currently use *Toolkit for Turbulence* as a leadership resource.

Frame	Focus	Find
Use the six-part structure of the book as a frame or canvas to plan your whole leadership toolkit. In addition, add your own favourite tools and any that catch your eye along the way.	Select one or more parts where you have a specific need. Leaders with new teams often begin with Part 4 'Team up' and add our ready-made models and tools to their team-building toolkit.	Treat the book as a 'go-to' resource whenever you need a tool to meet a personal, team or enterprise-wide challenge. The format of tools makes them easy to apply on the run.

It's up to you to choose the best way to build and maintain your leadership toolkit. We are confident that as you read the stories, test the tools and see the results you'll be able to build your own toolkit for turbulence. The only choice you can't make is to do nothing; your effectiveness as a leader will depend on it.

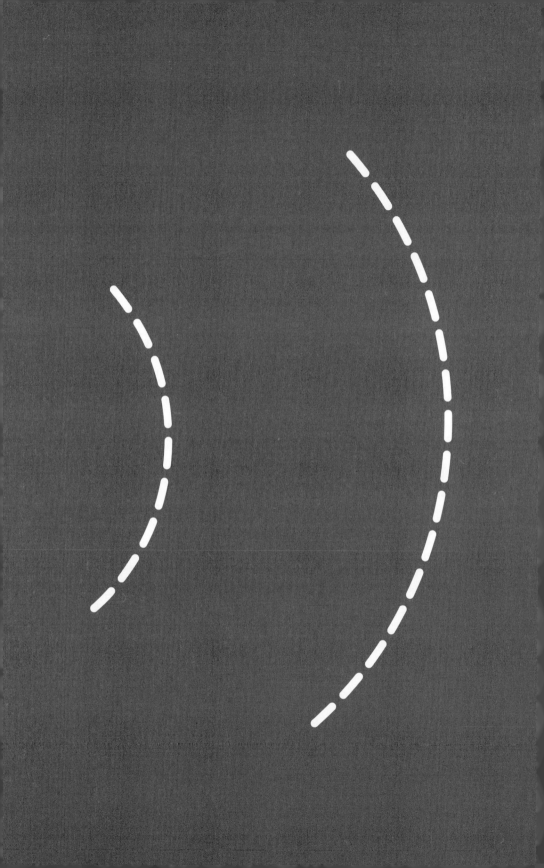

Pathway

... from disruption to advantage

In this opening part you will learn about the **pathway** from disruption through adaptation to advantage.

After reflecting on the nature of turbulence in your own world, you will learn three principles and priorities that are crucial to turning adversity into advantage: calibrate **mindset**, engage your **team** and be the **coach**.

You will hear stories from advantage leaders who have gone beyond just absorbing disruption and have built the capabilities and culture to become **versatile** enough to get stronger from tough experiences.

Then you will be ready to begin creating your own **toolkit for turbulence**!

CHAPTER 1

The moment

*'You must have chaos within you to give birth to
a dancing star.'*
Friedrich Nietzsche

Martin Bean: leaning into disruption

On 31 March 2020, the first of 263 days of COVID-19 lockdowns in
Melbourne, Australia, I was five years into the role of Vice Chancellor at
RMIT University, one of Australia's largest universities. ('Vice Chancellor'
is what universities like to call their Chief Executive Officer). As lockdown
began, I found myself pondering a big question: *What do you do when
over 11 000 staff and 80 000 students are relying on you as their leader, and
in your gut you fear your tried and tested leadership playbook is suddenly
made obsolete by a global pandemic?*

Let's be clear. I am not one to panic, and this wasn't my first rodeo. Half
a decade running The Open University, the largest university by number
of students in the United Kingdom, and General Manager of Worldwide
Education Products for Microsoft are two of many other leadership roles
I've filled. I know markets, finance and technology, my DNA is in leading
positive disruption at scale, and I can adapt as well as anyone. But this
was different.

To borrow the earthquake metaphor I'd learned from living in California,
this was 'the big one'.

The viability of a 133-year-old institution threatened by the complete
closure of campuses and borders. Thousands of students stranded.
Australia, Vietnam, Singapore, China all closed. Other universities
making rapid resolutions that could dramatically impact our options

and decisions. An unsympathetic federal government and a highly distracted state government.

Never to go back

If COVID-19 was the earthquake, then experience told me a tsunami would follow. Its name would be 'technology' and it would transform the world in unforeseen ways.

Microsoft Teams, Zoom and other collaboration tools, combined with accelerated automation, and generative artificial intelligence would forever change the workplace, while social media waves would amplify social causes and movements. At the time I really didn't give much thought to potential aftershocks that we now call supply chain shortages, energy crises, workforce and talent shortages, geopolitical uncertainty and volatile economic conditions. The world of work was changing and we'd never go back to the way it was before that day.

No plan survives first contact with the enemy

The world was a more predictable place when I joined RMIT University. This would be my last chief executive gig. An opportunity to bring together all I'd learned about developing leadership teams, running complex enterprises, and building cultures so people and technology could blend together to do great things. I intended to create a positive legacy that could be expressed in the five words that announced our RMIT University strategy: 'Ready for Life and Work'.

Whether it was Eisenhower, Rommel, Churchill or, more likely, Prussian Field Marshal Helmuth von Moltke who first famously pointed to the failure of the best-laid plans on first contact with the enemy, it certainly rang true for me on 31 March 2020.

What to do first?

I had my team set up a Microsoft Teams meeting with Graham Winter, an Australian psychologist we'd engaged to help me to build my executive team. I've always believed the most important task of a leader is to build and grow their team, and I intended my Vice Chancellor's Executive

(VCE) to be the best team of my career. I recruited outstanding talent and gave them time and resources to do the same in their teams.

My first contact with Graham had been a couple of years earlier at a meeting of Vice Chancellors where he'd skilfully facilitated a smart group of leaders with multiple agendas to find common ground and a breakthrough way forward. He had a style that helped make the complex simple. I assumed it reflected his diverse career experiences. He'd started in organisational psychology, then ventured into sport (even playing first-class cricket), with peak roles as Chief Psychologist to three Australian Olympic teams, then into a Big Four experience in the Asia Pacific region. For the past decade he had run his own business, Think One Team, which grew from authoring a best-selling book of the same name. His clients were top-performing leadership teams across defence, universities, government and corporate.

Unlike many psychologists, Graham used small words, and one caught my attention. That word was *tools*. He used it to describe the mental models and psychological skills athletes, business leaders and other high performers bring to achieve excellence in high-demand environments.

Positive disruption

I engaged Graham to help coach my executive team, and they responded well to his style and practical tools. A few months before COVID-19, Graham challenged me to reflect on whether I was really 'all in' on the desire for VCE to be the best team I'd ever led. He felt I was holding back — not surfacing some simmering tensions and wanting to keep things tidy and predictable.

'Martin, your team needs positive disruption to take them to the next level,' he warned. It was challenging to hear, but he was right. I needed to fight against my natural instincts as a 'peace maker' and to lean into the conflict, allowing the conversations that were needed. Looking back, it was then that the first seeds were sown for a way of thinking about myself, my team and my university that enabled us to turn the adversity of COVID-19 into advantage.

Graham Winter: finding the right moment

Martin is one of the best leaders I have worked with across my whole career in both the corporate world and elite sport. His superpower is to make people feel special, and he does that at scale across a room, an auditorium or even an online platform. He has that special connection with people that so often separates a good coach from a great coach.

Martin's playbook

When Martin first asked me to work with him and his team, I was excited by the opportunity to help shape an outstanding group of individuals into a high-performing team, and also the chance to learn from him. I quickly found why most of his team listed 'learning from Martin' as one of the attractions of their job.

What he called his 'playbook' was quite intimidating, because I often felt what I offered wasn't as good as what Martin could deliver by himself. Analysing this, I started to form a view that both Martin and I were holding back, albeit for different reasons.

I felt there was more Martin could give, more he wanted to give, and perhaps I wasn't the right person to partner with him to unlock that potential. We had a deep conversation, including about some of the contradictions of being a Chief Executive.

The gathering storm

Martin was like the admiral of the fleet torn between the responsibility to sail the charted course on which his enterprise had been travelling for more than 130 years and the sense that over the horizon was a gathering storm demanding not just a change of course but a rapid reset (if not transformation) of his ships and crews to suit completely different conditions.

We talked about leaders subconsciously seeking predictability and control, and why that wasn't surprising given the governance and culture pressures they felt every day.

Martin was attracted to leading-edge performance psychology and when we spoke about skills training for military, first responders and elite sport his eyes lit up as he wisely observed, 'They prepare to thrive in unpredictability while we do everything possible to eliminate it. That's why I need positive disruption, and so do my team. We just have to find the right moment.'

When Martin called on the first day of lockdown, I could tell he was as open to a new way as I'd ever known him.

'This is our moment, Graham,' he announced as I got familiar with the Microsoft Teams platform, which would become our primary channel of communication for the next 18 months.

And so we sketched out the model you see in the primary tool *The Pathway*. It became our first model and primary tool in the *Toolkit for Turbulence*. The statements next to each phase in the model capture our thinking.

Underpinning *The Pathway* were two well-known concepts:

» **Anti-fragility.** The term 'anti-fragile', coined and popularised by Nassim Taleb in his book of the same name, describes the characteristic of a system to get better from experiencing disorder.

» **VUCA (volatility, uncertainty, complexity, ambiguity).** VUCA originated as a concept in the 1980s and was brought to the world's attention by the US Army War College following the terror attacks of 9/11, when military planners found their conventional ways of planning, problem solving and managing risk were obsolete in an increasingly unpredictable and fast-changing world. Not surprisingly, the business world has embraced VUCA to describe their operating environment. We summarise that in one word, *turbulence*. Figure 1.1 (overleaf) offers a handy reference to business VUCA, including leadership risks.

The Pathway

The Pathway captures the essence of the approach taken by advantage leaders. This approach is born from necessity and underpinned by the two concepts of anti-fragility and VUCA (see table 1.1).

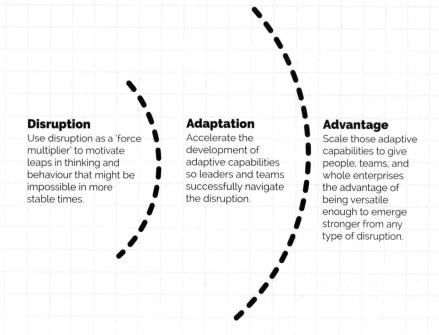

Disruption
Use disruption as a 'force multiplier' to motivate leaps in thinking and behaviour that might be impossible in more stable times.

Adaptation
Accelerate the development of adaptive capabilities so leaders and teams successfully navigate the disruption.

Advantage
Scale those adaptive capabilities to give people, teams, and whole enterprises the advantage of being versatile enough to emerge stronger from any type of disruption.

INSTRUCTIONS

The Pathway is referenced regularly in the book as a simple way to describe the three phases through which advantage leaders guide their teams.

Use the model as a tool for self-reflection and a conversation starter with your team and leadership colleagues. Here are some prompts:

» Where are the **creative opportunities** in disruption?

» How can we use this disruption to grow and strengthen **adaptive capabilities**?

» What's needed to scale these capabilities to enhance **versatility** for the whole enterprise?

VUCA	What's this about?	Business examples	Leadership risks
Volatility	The surprise factor of fast and unpredictable change	Stockmarkets, cyber-attacks and changing COVID-19 rules	Overreacting to threats; paralysed decision making
Uncertainty	Unpredictability is at the core of uncertainty, now and in the future	Supply chains, natural disasters, interest rate rises, disruptive technology	Too short term focused, stuck in minutiae, trying to control the uncontrollable
Complexity	Lots of factors interacting together in unpredictable ways	Global markets, organisational culture, climate change, media response to issues, increased governance intervention	Overwhelmed by scale, bogged down in analysis, oversimplification, lacking perspective
Ambiguity	The meaning of things is unclear or in conflict	Workplace paradoxes like profit and sustainability, short and long term, care for people and making tough calls	Rigid thinking about either/or, missing opportunities to innovate, avoidance thinking

Figure 1.1: outline of VUCA

Advantage leaders

Woven through *Toolkit for Turbulence* are quotes, stories and advice from experienced leaders about how they and their teams navigated the pathway from disruption through adaptation to advantage. All faced COVID-19, and each navigated the initial disruption and the turbulence that followed and continues to this day.

These are our co-creators and *advantage leaders*, because each can lay claim to having guided their team successfully along the Pathway. The varieties of turbulence they navigated helped shape the richness of their tools. We specifically sought out these leaders to contribute because they are exceptional people, and they represent a diverse spread of sectors and therefore types of turbulence.

Whether in defence, banking, aged care, health, technology, sport, energy, education, aviation, manufacturing, community services, major events, the arts, online employment or multiple tiers of government, our advantage leaders have confronted just about every form of VUCA and emerged stronger.

Andrew McConville, Chief Executive of the Murray–Darling Basin Authority, characterises the mindset of these leaders: 'I don't believe you can be a leader without accepting that you're going to have to deal with turbulence, or with uncertainty or volatility. That's why you sign up for the gig.'

Insights

Before moving on to explore *The Pathway* take the time to complete the insight exercise opposite.

We believe insights are one of the greatest accelerants of adaptability and a huge contributor to advantage. For a deeper dive into the concept of insights go to chapter 8, *Dial up the learning*.

INSIGHT EXERCISE
A brief stocktake of your current turbulence levels

How significant is the turbulence you are personally experiencing as a leader, and is it the same for your team?

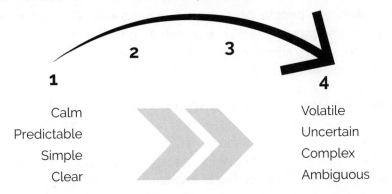

2   **3**

1   **4**

Calm   Volatile
Predictable   Uncertain
Simple   Complex
Clear   Ambiguous

In each of the four VUCA aspects, use the figure above to reflect on recent examples of turbulence you have faced or are facing.

» Which of the four VUCA elements are most impactful, and in what ways? For example, is complexity making prioritisation more challenging, or is uncertainty affecting workforce planning?

» Is your team experiencing anything different? If so, what is the effect for them and why is it different for you?

» What benefits are you looking to gain from *Toolkit for Turbulence* for yourself, your team and your wider enterprise?

Turning adversity to advantage

On a calm, clear day in 2008, just off the sparsely populated northwest coast of Australia, the fate of 315 passengers and crew on Qantas QF72 from Singapore to Perth lay in the hands of Captain Kevin Sullivan, a highly experienced pilot who had flown fighter jets in the US Navy and the Royal Australian Air Force.

They were cruising uneventfully at 11 000 metres when the onboard computers broadcast a series of confusing and contradictory signals before pitching the plane into two violent dives towards the Indian Ocean below, wrenching the pilots physically upwards from their seats and sending passengers and galley equipment crashing to the ceiling and back again.

More than 100 people were injured, many seriously, with fractures, lacerations and spinal injuries as the pilots fought for control of the Airbus A330-300, which, according to flight computers, was simultaneously stalling and over-speeding.

A later report would find a software error had caused the flight control computers to command the aircraft to pitch downward violently, wrenching control of the plane from Captain Sullivan and his crew. The automatic systems designed to make the plane safe had malfunctioned in a way that the pilots had not been trained to respond to. As Captain Sullivan wrote in his book *No Man's Land*, 'There is never any suggestion that the automation can fail… [because] there are enough back-up systems in place to cater for a wide range of failure situations.'

The pilots had only seconds to find an alternative to the pre-programmed 'playbook' that was hurling them earthward.

The 315 people on that plane owe their lives to Captain Sullivan's decisions and skills in taking back control of the plane and, after issuing mayday calls, landing the plane at remote Learmonth Airport (rather than risk the two hours to Perth), where they received emergency medical support from the first responders, the Royal Flying Doctor Service, CareFlight, the Western Australia Police Force and some generous members of the local community.

One of our advantage leaders, Kevin Sullivan shared in vivid detail how he wrested back control of his plane by falling back on leadership tools learned in US Navy training for a way out of what seemed an impossible situation.

'Everything is unprecedented until it happens for the first time,' observed another Sully, the equally heroic Captain Chesley Burnett 'Sully' Sullenberger III, captain of US Airways Flight 1549, which he landed without loss of life in the Hudson River after both engines were disabled by a bird strike.

How does this happen? How do pilots like Captains Sullivan and Sullenberger meet these unprecedented challenges by making superb team-oriented decisions when there is nothing but turbulence all around them? How do they cast aside conventional wisdom and playbooks to cobble together the tools they and their team need in the moment to turn adversity to advantage? And how can you replicate this approach in your leadership and with your team?

Learnings

» **Turbulence** is the mix of volatility, uncertainty, complexity and ambiguity (VUCA) affecting leaders, teams and enterprises worldwide.

» Embrace **positive disruption**. Disruption can be an opportunity to turn adversity into advantage provided you are willing to embrace disruption, lean into conflict and allow for the conversations that need to happen.

» The COVID-19 pandemic has **accelerated** the adoption of advanced technology and has forever changed the world of work.

» The **Pathway model** describes three phases: *disruption*, *adaptation* and *advantage*. *Toolkit for Turbulence* shows how top leaders use disruption as a catalyst for change and develop adaptive capabilities to emerge stronger from any type of turbulence.

» Embrace **anti-fragility**. While conventional wisdom advises us to build resilience to withstand disruption, an anti-fragile mindset seeks to get stronger from the experience.

» Throughout the book you will learn from **leaders** in a diverse spread of sectors who have experienced many different types of turbulence and emerged as advantage leaders.

CHAPTER 2

Advantage leader

How do advantage leaders approach a disruption such as COVID-19? What mindsets help or hinder? How do they sustain their own and their team's performance and wellbeing? What have they learned and taken forward? What did they leave behind? What's new in their playbook, or do they even have a playbook?

The accelerant

Everyone experienced COVID-19, and that's why The Pathway begins there, although it's not the only reason. We also start there because the pandemic became a force multiplier of change in workplace mindsets and behaviours that might have taken years to develop in other circumstances.

Early in the pandemic Martin described COVID-19 as 'an accelerant with the potential to supercharge the adoption of technology in a way that would disrupt the world of work forever'. It was no exaggeration. There's no going back to the ways of work of early 2020, no matter how much some people might miss past habits and routines.

Here's a snapshot of what happened:

» In the blink of an eye, Microsoft Teams and Zoom enabled millions of people displaced and isolated by the virus to connect and continue working away from the office, most never to return to the old ways.

» A boom in e-commerce washed over the economy, leaving cash-and-carry retailing in its wake.

» Telemedicine and online education took a giant leap into a new digital age, changing hundreds of years of mainstream practice in weeks.

» Vaccines were developed and distributed in timeframes unthinkable two years earlier.

» People's attitude to work fundamentally changed, and the war for talent ignited.

» The impact of social media and digital activism expanded as the shifting generational mix led by Millennials and Generation Z took stronger positions on the big social, environmental and political dilemmas.

» Disruption piled on top of disruption as borders closed, a war broke out in Ukraine clogging supply chains and government spending added fuel to the fire of inflation.

COVID-19 unquestionably changed the dynamics of the world of work. While most leaders had hitherto faced the usual array of business ups and downs, this was like climbing into the largest roller coaster ever built and being catapulted forward without warning.

In-the-field experience

To whet your appetite for the breadth of experiences you will enjoy throughout the book, here are two examples from our advantage leaders.

On Friday, 13 March 2020, with a crowd in excess of 70 000 expected and thousands queuing before the gates had opened at Albert Park, Melbourne, Andrew Westacott, CEO of the Australian Grand Prix Corporation, stood resolutely adjacent to the International Media Centre to announce to the world's media the first COVID-19-related cancellation of a major international sporting event. Just five days earlier 80 000 people had crammed the MCG to watch the Australia women's cricket team win the World Cup. For 45 minutes Andrew and Formula 1® stakeholders, with whom he'd built the deep relationships needed to work in sync under pressure, fielded question after question live from the world's media. Little did they know that it would be two years before another Formula 1® Grand Prix would be held in Australia, and this would present them with an extraordinary set of challenges to navigate.

Bernadette McDonald, now CEO of The Royal Children's Hospital Melbourne, was leading the Canberra Health Services in early 2020. 'It looked like a tsunami coming towards us, with patients taking up our beds, but also potentially no workforce. I was running the hospital, reporting to two ministers and a chief minister and a cabinet, and had to provide the reassurance — "We've got this", "We'll be okay", "What are we doing?", "How many ventilators do we need?" — while also dealing with the media.'

Andrew Westacott, Bernadette McDonald and all the advantage leaders now point to experiences during the turbulence of COVID-19 as game-changing for themselves, their teams and their organisations. There is no formula for what they did. Each used their own unique leadership tools and techniques. However, the principles are remarkably similar to those we adopted in the early days of the pandemic and applied successfully with the VCE team.

Those principles, and stories of the tools and techniques applied across a vast range of industries and sectors, provide a wonderful guide for any leader who recognises that we now live in the age of disruption.

The toolkit

What Martin called his 'playbook' was not a document to read and follow but rather a metaphor for the beliefs, tools and tactics accumulated over a career of diverse leadership experiences.

When COVID-19 hit, it was entirely understandable that he should feel disoriented, because many of the assumptions underpinning the way he had learned to lead his team and enterprise had just flown out the window.

Staff were no longer physically in the workplace, revenue targets were unachievable with students locked out of their campuses and of Australia, volatility made planning unreliable at best, basic community freedoms were suspended, and the physical and psychological wellbeing of all staff —including the most senior leaders—was quickly becoming a major concern.

It was time to challenge the mental model of a 'playbook' and replace it with something fit for purpose.

The main problem wasn't the content of the playbook. It makes sense to reduce complexity by applying a range of 'set plays'. The risk was in going back to plans and tactics that had been developed as the 'right way' to lead in a context that had vastly changed and showed every sign of continuing to do so.

It was like a tennis coach having a playbook for the clay courts of Roland Garros and using that to prepare for Wimbledon.

COVID-19 upended conventional wisdom. The mainstays of business— strategic planning, annual operating plans and budgets, organisational hierarchy, HR practices and process flow charts — all assumed a level of linear predictability and a 'right' answer. They were very much like the clay court playbook, designed for an environment where things happen more slowly and in a more predictable sequence.

Playbooks have great value. However, if you are piloting an out-of-control plane or facing a cyber-attack that shuts down a national stock exchange for a week at the height of COVID-19, you can understand why a leader like the New Zealand Stock Exchange's CEO, Mark Peterson, should have remarked bluntly, 'You throw out the playbook when you get something like that.'

Mental models

Martin didn't throw out his playbook, and neither did our advantage leaders. Instead they selected the most useful tools and invented more, because in disruption context is king, which means using what works *in the moment.*

Captain Kevin Sullivan offers a perfect example.

Trained in the US Navy, he had learned to calibrate his mindset to stay calm, and in the moment, so he could problem solve effectively in high-stakes situations. His mental toolkit included a simple and powerful three-point mental model: 'Aviate – Navigate – Communicate'. It had been drilled into him through endless disciplined feedback loops and the mantra *Leader First, Pilot Second*, which reinforced his responsibility to lead.

'Aviate' was the number one priority. It required maintaining control and altitude of the aircraft: 'You must maintain the aircraft in a safe flight path, and that takes priority'. 'Navigate' came next, with a focus on problem-solving options for the plane, including choosing an emergency landing site rather than risking taking seriously injured passengers and a malfunctioning plane on to Perth. Once those decisions were made, it was time to 'communicate' with air traffic control and others regarding identity, location and situation.

Most of the tools in *Toolkit for Turbulence* are mental models, which combined together form a sort of mental scaffolding (a toolkit) that can be drawn on in any situation to help analyse and solve problems. *Aviate – Navigate – Communicate* is just one example; you will no doubt already have many mental models that help you make sense of the world and inform how you lead. Pilots, nurses, engineers, train drivers, electricians, photographers and of course leaders all use mental models to navigate complexity. The better your scaffolding of mental models, the better your ability to learn and problem solve.

Graham Winter: reimagine and reset

QF72 offered an all-too-graphic illustration of shifting from linear thinking (follow the Airbus SE processes) to a more fluid, in-the-moment learning and problem-solving model, by using and adapting whatever mental models (tools) that can be applied to move forward safely and successfully.

Elite athletes, the military and first responders train for this adaptive style of thinking and decision making. Not that they aren't also drilled in the knowledge and practices of playbooks, but in high-stakes environments knowledge doesn't equal leadership. In those conditions safety and success depend on a composed and clear mind, adaptive leadership and cohesive teamwork. They trust in the toolkit of mental skills and techniques they and their team have honed, and they choose what's needed in the moment.

In March 2020, with precious little time and exponentially growing threats, Martin saw the need and opportunity to reimagine and reset his leadership approach to guide his team and enterprise from disruption to advantage.

My advice, based on decades of working with some of the world's best coaches, athletes and business leaders in high-stakes environments, was clear and pragmatic: 'Think about your playbook as an evolving toolkit and focus on three priorities: first, calibrate your mindset; second, engage your team to "build, test and learn" a new toolkit; third, be the coach your people need.'

Each of those priorities is a principle backed by evidence and experience in performance psychology:

» *Calibrate your mindset* means embracing turbulence by adapting your attitudes, beliefs and assumptions to meet challenges as they emerge.

» *Engage your team to build, test and learn* means becoming a cohesive and nimble team that aligns, collaborates, learns and delivers at pace.

» *Be the coach your people need* means accepting full personal responsibility for unlocking the potential of every team member and the team as a whole.

In March 2020 we discussed, debated and committed to a new way forward. It was to build, test, learn and refine a *toolkit for turbulence* for Martin and his team, who would collectively lead over 11 000 staff and 80 000 students through and beyond the pandemic.

As illustrated in figure 2.1, it meant focusing on the three core principles.

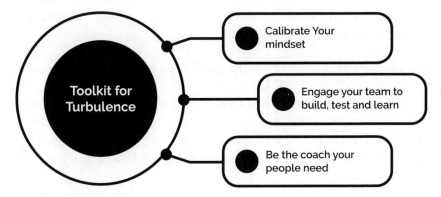

Figure 2.1: the three core principles

The three principles

Why did these three principles matter for Martin and VCE? What did each principle mean in practical terms when disruption was everywhere? When and how did they also emerge in the stories and experiences of advantage leaders? Why do they matter for you?

The three principles frame the key parts of this book. Each is crucial to the *Pathway*: to initially navigate the intensity of disruption from COVID-19 and subsequent turbulence, to build the personal and team capabilities for adaptation, and to lock in the habits and culture that repeatedly turn adversity to advantage.

Principle 1. Calibrate your mindset

Of all the potential tools and capabilities, one stands out as most important to turning adversity to advantage. An adaptive mindset is the key to combatting something we all experience in tough conditions: *a defensive or protective mindset.*

An adaptive mindset sees the opportunities in changing and tough conditions and allows us to respond constructively and flexibly. 'Leaders must deal with the uncertainty of today whilst picking their head up and looking at where the growth and the opportunity is,' advises advantage leader Robert Iervasi, formerly Group CEO of Asahi Beverages, Oceania Region, one of the leading beverage companies in Australia and New Zealand and employer of nearly 4000 people.

There's a second aspect to mindset, which we'll briefly introduce here.

Imagine you are driving through the busy, jumbled streets of Mumbai. Where do you focus your attention? How do you navigate the endlessly changing streetscape? Could you plan your way through the journey? Imagine what would happen if you turned to gesture angrily at the driver who just cut you off.

Exactly, you'd crash! You might conclude that it was simply impossible to drive in Mumbai. And you might be right, but chances are you could become a good Mumbai driver if you were to consider recalibrating your mindset or, in other words, making a paradigm shift.

This paradigm shift might mean challenging and quite possibly changing your assumptions about driving a car. Assumptions like driving on one side of the road, indicating before changing direction, giving way at intersections and only overtaking when it is clear ahead!

The term *paradigm shift*, coined by Thomas Kuhn, a twentieth-century scientist, is perfectly apt for describing many of the big shifts that are part of turbulence. Some are obvious, like shifting from office-based working to hybrid and remote working, from bricks and mortar to clicks and mortar, and from on-premise IT systems to cloud-based systems. Others, such as leadership styles, strategic planning and organisation design, are somewhat less visible but nevertheless point towards the need to recalibrate mindset to successfully lead in the workplace of today.

In *Toolkit for Turbulence*, you will learn how to shift and shape your paradigms by deep diving into four specific shifts or recalibrations that are common along the pathway:

> » **Anchor on personal values** is a shift to anchoring your decisions in deeply held personal values, because when all the 'rules' are

stripped away you need a framework for authentic and effective communication and decision making.

»   ***Embrace the externality of change*** means learning new ways to navigate uncertainty and ambiguity and to move through the transitions that are inevitable in an age of disruption.

»   ***Dial up the learning*** is a call to shift the pace and style of your personal learning to match the imperative to adapt quickly.

»   ***Prioritise self-care*** reinforces the point that personal wellbeing matters and requires you to pay attention to your own needs so you are equipped to lead others through adversity.

The VUCA elements (volatility, uncertainty, complexity, ambiguity) can each present potential threats to your sense of certainty, control and belonging, and can throw mindsets into protection and defensive mode. When that happens, you might react aggressively and be overly competitive and controlling, or go too passive to avoid conflict and risk.

These are natural human reactions. However, as Robert Iervasi notes, 'Leaders who don't snap themselves out of reactive mode and into proactive response plus growth, are really going to struggle.'

Mindset absolutely matters when facing turbulence, and that's why we will show you how to recognise your own defensive reactions, to challenge and shift paradigms, and to pivot toward the adaptive mindset that is proven as a key to thriving in conditions of challenge and change.

Principle 2. Engage your team to build, test and learn a new toolkit

Care Connect Group is one of Australia's largest independent providers of in-home aged care. CEO Paul Ostrowski has led the organisation for over a decade. In recent years, however, he and his team have found themselves in the eye of the proverbial 'perfect storm'.

When Paul speaks about turbulence, he goes back to before COVID-19, recounting the impacts of a royal commission on an industry beset by ever-changing funding models and regulations. And then there are the stories of staff and clients battered by COVID-19, devastating bushfires and floods, and of workforce shortages throwing the industry into crisis.

Balancing day-to-day operational challenges with a substantial transformation agenda has pushed his leadership team to the limit. 'My team has juggled almost every imaginable challenge over the past three years, not the least being the wellbeing and performance of a wonderful but very stretched workforce.'

Keen to turn disruption to advantage, Paul engaged his team to test and learn a new operating rhythm based on one of the primary tools in *Toolkit for Turbulence*. That tool, called 'ACL', helps teams to *align*, *collaborate* and *learn* at pace in complex and volatile operating environments.

ACL is just one example of the *loop and learn* approach employed by most teams in high-demand environments. For example, a group of first responders will *align* around purpose, goals and immediate priorities, *collaborate* to explore and solve problems, and *learn* in the moment and later by debriefing. Then they'll adapt and 'spin the ACL' again. You will learn more about ACL in chapter 10; it provides the blueprint for Part 4, *Team up*.

Principle 3. Be the coach your people need

Why was it a priority for Martin to *be the coach his people needed*? A prime reason was because COVID-19 lockdowns triggered an emotion-charged environment where every member was stretched to — perhaps even beyond — their personal limits. The days quickly became an intense, rolling series of challenges: distressed staff, displaced at-risk students, technologies stretched to breaking point, and life-changing financial and people decisions. And of course, all the team had families experiencing the first pandemic in a century.

A team facing prolonged turbulence is almost assured of failures, of being exposed, of having basic beliefs and assumptions shaken, and of having to fly blind at times. They need a leader who cares about them and whom they trust, so they can lean into the discomfort without overly protecting themselves or holding back.

Bernadette McDonald explains: 'You have to bring understanding and a deep empathy for people, especially when they are facing the unknown and experiencing anxiety. It's essential to provide reassurance, even though you aren't sure, because you still have to give people confidence that together we'll do what's best and we'll work our way through, and we'll learn together.'

Be the coach means creating spaces of psychological safety and courage so people can show up as their best selves and get comfortable with the inevitable setbacks and failures.

During the pandemic Melbourne earned the title of the world's most locked down city, which put Melbourne's Lord Mayor, Sally Capp AO, and her team at the epicentre of disruption. 'Balancing the health priorities with the mental, emotional, economic, physical consequences of lockdown was really, really tough.'

To be the coach her people needed, Sally describes being more open to failure and risk than ever before and personally owning the inevitable mistakes. And she walked the talk, in 2021 standing in front of a press pack searching for answers to why Moomba 2021 was cancelled and admitting, 'I got it wrong.' To those challenged by such openness her reply is clear: 'In my gut, I had to say, "We got it wrong," because we got it wrong. I had no justification. There were lots of reasons I could use as excuses, but at the end of the day, I didn't think that it cut the mustard.' That's setting an example, and that's what people need from their coach in tough times.

The coach people need accepts they are fully accountable for their team; for their wellbeing, development and effectiveness, collectively and individually. A key to that accountability is to ensure the team have the tools to successfully navigate turbulence and even gain advantage from it.

Encouragement

Turbulence might upend your leadership and team journey, but it doesn't have to end in crash and burn.

History shows that Martin and his VCE team embraced ambiguity and successfully navigated through almost unimaginable disruption. *Toolkit for Turbulence* evolved with the input of our wonderful advantage leaders, a few of whom you've already met briefly in this chapter, to become a treasure trove of insights into the mindsets, tools and practices that have guided leaders and teams through all manner of disruption, to emerge not just intact but ahead because they have built the capabilities and culture to turn adversity to advantage.

Learnings

» COVID-19 is the once-in-a-lifetime disruptor that **accelerated** changes in workplace mindsets and behaviours that might have taken years to emerge in other circumstances.

» Advantage leaders didn't throw out their playbooks in the pandemic. They did select and **adapt** tools, because in disruption context is king, which means using what works in the moment.

» To lead through disruption and turn it to your advantage, follow these three principles:

  » **Calibrate your mindset** by embracing turbulence and adapting your attitudes, beliefs and assumptions to meet challenges as they emerge.

  » **Engage your team to build, test and learn** by becoming a cohesive and nimble team that aligns, collaborates, learns and delivers at pace.

  » **Be the coach your people need** by accepting full responsibility to unlock the potential of every team member and the team as a whole.

» Turbulence might upend your leadership and team journey, but it doesn't have to end in crash and burn. You can develop the mindset, toolkit and coaching skills to be **effective** in whatever turbulence comes at you and your team.

2

Mindset

*... from defensive
to adaptive*

In Part 1 you learned about advantage leaders and the unique **pathway** they take to equip themselves and their team for turbulence. You also reflected on the meaning and impacts of turbulence in your world. In Part 2 you'll start working on your mindset by first exploring the nature and implications of **linear and nonlinear challenges** and secondly strengthening your **adaptive mindset**, because it's the 'secret sauce' for turning adversity to advantage.

CHAPTER 3

Linear versus nonlinear

What challenges do disruption and turbulence present? What is the nature of these challenges? Are they fundamentally the same or different? If the challenges are different, how will you know and what does it mean for leadership and teamwork?

Context shapes us

Have you ever wondered how different you would be if you had grown up in a completely different environment? How you might think differently about life? How your values, habits and skills would have evolved as you adapted to a vastly different world?

Imagine for a moment you were born a Bedouin hundreds of years ago in the Arabian Peninsula. Your family and nomadic tribe face life-and-death challenges in the scorching summers and freezing nights, eking out a marginal existence from scarce and hidden food, water and shelter.

Stand still on the ever-shifting sand and your feet sink, so you keep moving. Every step is different as you climb dune after dune and beyond. As a Bedouin your walking style has adapted to this world, finding an optimal pace between going too slowly and sinking and pushing too deep from moving too fast. Your clothing is adapted too. You most likely wear a *thawb*, an ankle-length gown with wide sleeves like wings that have great functionality for everything from carrying children to signifying tribal status.

To find your way you learn to rely not on footsteps in the sand but rather on static features such as mountain peaks, large rocks and valleys as navigation points, and when needed you add your own markers and signs that enable you to chart a course safely.

Among the shifting dunes and vast flat basins that give rise to glimmering mirages, you find patterns above and below. You can set your course by the sun's path during the day and at night by the map of stars etched into your imagination. The ground also gives clues to the direction of the wind as it shapes the dunes, forming them at 90 degrees to the prevailing wind. You didn't learn this at school; experience alone taught you that a prevailing wind from the east creates dunes running north to south.

You live your life, like humans have throughout history, facing and adapting to the changes and challenges of your world, from wolves and vipers to storms and drought.

In the modern world your challenges are unlikely to include volatile and uncertain sand fields, complex, ever-changing desert patterns, or ambiguous mirages with their mixed messages of hope and disappointment. You pay little heed to sinking sand and desert heat, yet you face the same basic need to adapt to the challenges of volatility, uncertainty, complexity and ambiguity.

These challenges are of two basic types, linear and nonlinear, and your ability to distinguish between the two, and to successfully address both, is as essential to navigating the pathway from disruption to advantage as were the Bedouin's skills to navigating a confusing desert landscape.

Know your challenges

How many management and leadership theories and models have been introduced to the business world over the past 50 years? The answer no doubt runs in the thousands, but one stands out as the essential starting point for understanding the challenges of a turbulent world.

The distinction between 'technical' and 'adaptive' challenges was identified by Ronald Heifetz from Harvard University in the 1990s when he observed leaders struggling with persistent and complex problems. He particularly noticed that their methods of problem solving, which they had applied successfully to technical issues like fixing machinery and installing systems, were ill suited to more complex and ambiguous settings where the issues were more about people and culture.

More recently the terms *linear* and *nonlinear* have replaced *technical* and *adaptive* in day-to-day leadership conversations. The underlying premise remains the same, however, you need different tools (mental models) to deal with complex or nonlinear challenges because, as we will explore, they present adaptive challenges. This insight reveals three crucial capabilities that are the starting point for building a toolkit for turbulence:

» **Notice** the differences between linear and nonlinear challenges.

» **Adapt** your approach to these challenges.

» **Apply** different tools to suit the nature of these challenges.

By correctly identifying a challenge as either linear or nonlinear, you can not only apply the best approach to your own problem solving and leadership, but also help your team to better understand their role and how their contribution makes a difference.

Capability 1. Notice the differences

The differences between linear and nonlinear problems are reasonably easy to spot if you are alert to the signs; however, most of your challenges will have both, which adds a degree of difficulty.

Here are the basic differences:

Linear problems have a known or logical solution. They can be simple, like assembling an Ikea chair, or complicated, like the electronics in your car, but they have a common feature: they can be analysed and solved in a logical way using expert knowledge. They are predictable and people generally accept the solution because there is 'best practice' and they tend to trust experts. Life is somewhat calmer and more predictable when most problems are linear, because you can organise your experts into structures and roles where they know the boundaries and what's expected of them to solve the challenges.

Nonlinear problems lack a known solution. It's often difficult to define the actual problem, let alone the solution. Think of any challenge that requires people to adopt new ways of working, such as hybrid working or virtual teams, and you are looking at a nonlinear challenge. The solution requires people to be open to talking about and defining the real nature of the problem, to experiment and learn together, and to change their attitudes, beliefs and habits. Nonlinear problems are unpredictable and can stir up emotions because they are uncertain and challenge assumptions and beliefs; in addition, they often involve uncomfortable trade-offs.

A recent example of challenges having both linear and nonlinear elements is the explosion in the use of generative artificial intelligence (GenAI), such as ChatGPT and DALL-E 2, and the impact on schools and universities. Suddenly students have immediate free access to a technology that can write essays and create images, videos, and 3D models. The potential impact on coursework and assessments drew immediate reactions, with some institutions trying to block use and access. This clearly has significant nonlinear elements, as described in the following primary tool, *Recognise linear and nonlinear problems*.

Recognise linear and nonlinear problems

Whenever you encounter challenges in the workplace look for the five signs in the model shown.

Notice how the problems on the left are predictable in nature — in other words, there is a clear link between cause and effect. Those on the right side are more complex and less predictable.

Linear problem	⬤	Nonlinear problem
Well-defined problem	**1**	Hard-to-define problem
Clear, practical solution	**2**	Unclear or unknown solution
Requires narrow expertise	**3**	Requires collaboration
Mainly about processes, systems and technologies	**4**	Mainly about people: assumptions, beliefs and/or habits
Clear ending — equilibrium	**5**	Ongoing attention needed

INSTRUCTIONS

1. Take a few moments to jot down five to seven leadership challenges you are currently facing or see on the horizon.

2. Weigh each of the problems against the five signs in this model to identify the linear and nonlinear elements.

   » To what extent are your challenges linear or nonlinear?

   » Can you see both linear and nonlinear elements in the same challenge?

   » What do you sense are the leadership implications of those differences?

Keep a copy of this model and use it as a reference.

Be alert to the nature of challenges

Strengths can become weaknesses when the context shifts, and failing to make the distinction between linear and nonlinear challenges is a common reason why.

From her leadership experience in universities and more recently in defence science, Professor Tanya Monro AC, Australia's Chief Defence Scientist and leader of Defence Science and Technology Group, has observed how the mindsets and habits of scientists to favour deep analysis and find 'right answers' serves them well for complicated challenges. However, in volatility and complexity these habits and mindsets get in the way of what she calls 'finding the best answers for the context'.

This need to give up on 'right answers' and instead develop the 'best answers for the context' highlights why adaptability is so crucial to navigating turbulent (nonlinear) conditions.

Paul Duldig was Chief Operating Officer at the Australian National University throughout the pandemic. Asked how he found solutions to the most complex and ambiguous challenges, his reply offers a great insight into the way context shapes an advantage leader's thinking: 'Nonlinearity is key. Don't get caught up in whether it makes sense just because it's what you did in the past, or if the direct result doesn't necessarily stack up, because in disruption the effects aren't linear. You have to make judgement calls on risk and return, and then learn really quickly and pivot if needed.'

Being alert to nonlinear challenges is essential because these challenges require adapting, not first finding a right answer.

Capability 2. Adapt your approach

Each of the five signs of linear versus nonlinear problems provides a hint as to how to adapt your thinking and behaviour to tackle complex issues. In figure 3.1 we take the five signs and unpack some of the implications of nonlinear challenges for your thinking and leadership practices.

The challenge	How to adapt your thinking and behaviour
Hard-to-define problem	Take time to listen, explore and get clear on what it is you are trying to solve before you start solving it. **Key leadership question:** *What exactly is the core problem?*
Unclear or unknown solution	Avoid jumping quickly to solutions without first defining the problem and looking at it from multiple perspectives. **Key leadership question:** *What alternative solutions could we consider?*
Requires collaboration	Nonlinear challenges need input from multiple stakeholders, so seek to bring the optimal expertise, experience and perspectives. **Key leadership question:** *Who can contribute here to bring diverse and valuable insights?*
Mainly about people	Reflect on what changes are going to be needed in people's habits and in their underlying assumptions and beliefs to effectively meet the challenge. **Key leadership question:** *What changes are needed in people's mindset and behaviour (and from which people)?*
Ongoing attention needed	While linear problems are usually 'fixed', nonlinear problems often need ongoing monitoring and attention. **Key leadership question:** *What's going to be needed to sustain positive change?*

Figure 3.1: implications of nonlinear challenges

Capability 3. Apply different tools

Imagine two leaders in a regional community health centre, both planning to implement a new rostering system developed by head office in response to a customer engagement survey. The new roster will create a lot of change for staff, such as shifting from a 9.00 to 5.30 single-location clinic model to multiple clinics and telehealth arrangements, including being open 12 hours a day and on Saturday mornings. There will be reasonable increases in staffing numbers to accommodate the extended hours; however, it will require a rearrangement of teams into flexible multidisciplinary pods supported by small administration teams and a central help desk.

Leader A treats this as a linear problem and proceeds to work with the two most senior supervisors on a detailed spreadsheet that maps the staff hours to the new customer hours and locations. They do a superb job of creating a new framework that will ensure all hours are serviced by the right cross-sections of allied health and administrative staff. In addition, they decide to implement a new software system to give people visibility of their team and times across sites and via telehealth. Confident of their work, they email all staff with the plan and schedule a meeting for later in the week to answer any questions prior to implementation the following month.

Leader B treats this as a nonlinear problem and gathers their leadership team together to talk about the head office plan, the insights and recommendations from the study and the implications. They agree the dual aim is to achieve an optimal service for customers and an optimal working environment for staff. Moving quickly, they check in with head office to confirm expectations. From those discussions they learn there is potential flexibility in the timing and approach to achieve the required service standards. Armed with the customer study and options, they convene initial briefing sessions for staff and commit to providing an opportunity to co-create the next steps. A sub-group of staff and leaders then design three scenarios to meet the customer and staff needs. Based on ideas from short online workshop sessions with staff, it is agreed to run a pilot at one service hub using a multidisciplinary approach. Over the following month staff and leaders gather insights from the pilot and settle on a flexible system that most of the staff support.

The most common leadership failure

You might have guessed that this was largely a real-life scenario, though the people and organisation are not identified for obvious reasons. The amazing thing is that three months from the head office edict, Leader B effectively had the whole workforce committed to operating in the way Leader A had described on their spreadsheet. Leader A, however, ended up in an industrial dispute with claims of bullying and stress, and ultimately moved to another position after people actively resisted attempts to implement change with little consultation.

Heifetz and colleagues famously wrote, 'The most common leadership failure stems from trying to apply technical solutions to adaptive challenges.'

You've no doubt seen it happen. The rush to a technical solution (employing a linear mindset) when the challenge needs a more adaptive, nonlinear approach, open to experimenting and learning, and willing to co-create and settle for the 'imperfect solution'.

Recalling the challenges confronting the Australian National University during the pandemic, Paul Duldig observes, 'While the natural tendency in universities is to take a hierarchical approach to decision making, we saw advantage in pushing it in the other direction and going much more decentralised because of the incredibly adaptive nature of the challenge, and that worked really well.'

Beware the dragons

Why is it so counterproductive to take a linear approach to a nonlinear problem?

There are no guarantees that taking a nonlinear approach will result in success. However, there are four big 'dragons' (see figure 3.2, overleaf) that can seriously upset your plans to move along the pathway, and it seems that taking a more linear approach often fires up those dragons.

Be on the lookout for these 'dragons', because they are a helpful reminder for you to create an environment where people work together to address the complex nonlinear challenges and not just execute a more linear solution through the hierarchy or some experts in silos.

Mistrust. While linear problems can sometimes be solved without relationships, complex challenges need people to be open and work together. Mistrust makes this difficult and derails problem solving.	**Power and politics.** The dynamics of status and power have probably blocked more change attempts than they have helped, and if people feel they are being made less important they'll likely prove that's not the case by blocking progress.
Resistance to change. Despite the imperative to change, people resist for a host of reasons, such as fear, uncertainty and loss of control. Hierarchical decisions add to resistance, as do solutions imposed under the guise of 'expert opinion'.	**Conflict.** Complex challenges are often emotionally charged, and this makes it difficult to have constructive conversations. Often a linear solution is adopted just to quell the short-term emotions, but it doesn't resolve the underlying issue.

Figure 3.2: the four dragons of nonlinear challenges

Alert your team to the nonlinear

What are the big challenges facing your team now and over the coming months? Will they recognise whether these are linear or nonlinear challenges? Do they have the mindset and skills to successfully lean into the complex challenges?

Strengthening your team's ability to notice and act on the differences between linear and nonlinear challenges can improve their problem solving, communication and capacity to transition through change.

By understanding the nature of the challenges, they will be better able to choose the best approach to problem solving and to communicate effectively, which can contribute to resilience and adaptability.

Team talk. Be alert to the nonlinear

Use this tool as a team activity to help your team to recognise the vital distinction between linear and nonlinear, and to apply the right mindset and skills to the right problems.

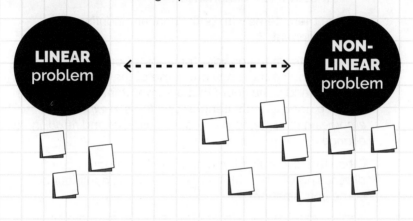

INSTRUCTIONS

1. Explain and discuss why team members will benefit from a shared approach to tackling the most important business problems and challenges.

2. Provide Post-it notes or their online equivalent and ask each member to write down some of the key challenges they are facing in their work.

3. Use the linear–nonlinear model to explain the nature of linear and nonlinear problems and highlight the key differences

4. Ask members to take it in turns to share their challenges and place them along a continuum from linear to nonlinear (use a wall if you are in a room together)

(continued)

5. When everyone has placed their Post-its, facilitate a discussion:

   » What does the spread of items tell us?

   » What characteristics led to the conclusion that an item is mostly linear or nonlinear?

   » Are there items with both linear and nonlinear components?

6. Guide the team to consider the implications for their mindset and habits. Draw out some of the characteristic attitudes and behaviours that are important when dealing with the nonlinear challenges: *openness to experiment, embracing challenges, co-creating solutions* and *flexibility to change.*

7. Close the discussion by reinforcing the importance of diagnosing whether challenges are linear, nonlinear or some combination.

Recap

Most significant workplace challenges have nonlinear components, or in other words they don't have a clearly defined problem and a predictable solution. Instead, they are complex and ambiguous, and are likely to challenge and require change to people's assumptions, beliefs and habits. This fundamentally changes the way the problem needs to be addressed.

The time invested in guiding your team to get better at recognising linear and nonlinear challenges will be valuable in avoiding wasted time and effort developing technical solutions to far more complex problems.

Learnings

» By correctly identifying the **linear** or **nonlinear** aspects of challenges you can apply the best approach to your own problem solving and help your team to better understand how to make a positive impact.

» Distinguish between a linear and nonlinear challenge by examining whether the problem and solution are clear, if it is primarily about **things or people**, and whether it can be fully 'fixed' by an expert or might need ongoing attention.

» To successfully address nonlinear challenges clarify the problem, be open to exploring and experimenting, facilitate **collaboration** and give attention to sustaining the outcome.

» A common leadership mistake is to treat problems as linear when they are more **complex**, which results in the real problems going unresolved.

» It can be hard to navigate through **adaptive change** because it is nonlinear, but don't make it harder by allowing mistrust, power, politics, conflict or resistance to get in the way.

CHAPTER 4

Defeat the defensive mindset

With an adaptive mindset we see opportunities among challenging and tough conditions. We respond constructively with courage, flexibility and openness to learn, and we engage with others to find creative ways forward.

Superpower

Do you find a turbulent environment stimulating or overwhelming?

Of course, that's a ridiculous question. You might find it to be both, neither or more likely some combination in between, because every situation is different.

Trying to predict how you or your team might think and act in response to volatile and uncertain events isn't easy, which makes it harder to prepare. However, performance psychology research and practice tell us that it starts with an adaptive mindset.

An adaptive mindset equips you and your team to deal with fast and unpredictable change, to navigate in uncertainty, to collaborate on complex entangled problems, and to embrace ambiguity and paradoxes.

That means before you think about strategies and tools, your priority is to understand adaptive mindset principles and how the associated tools can help you to live and lead effectively in high-demand environments. Without them, you risk your feelings and focus being thrown around like a lifeboat in a stormy sea.

Turbulence presents a high-demand environment for leaders and teams, which means the essential first step in preparing for these conditions is to strengthen their adaptive mindset.

Defensive or adaptive?

Tanya Monro leads in one of the most complex and high-stakes environments in the world. Her team of more than 2000 employees work at the leading edge of defence science and technology. Most are highly trained scientists, technologists and professionals, yet when asked, 'What is most important to enable success for the organisation?', it is not the deep technical skills she singles out but mindset: 'Success often comes down to shifting mindsets from protective and defensive into seeing the opportunities in change.'

You and your team will want to lean into the challenges of turbulence and, as Tanya suggests, 'see the opportunities in change'. There's a big question mark on that, though, and it has little to do with technical skills or know-how; it's the very natural human tendency to respond to threats everywhere.

And it gets worse! Think for a moment about the daily stream of breaking news and news alerts from all forms of media. We are effectively being trained to see threats everywhere.

That's important to be aware of, because you and your team are being fed a daily training regime that goes in exactly the opposite direction to where you want to go! It is a significant barrier to personal and team effectiveness, because with a defensive mindset your thinking is cautious and fixed, and you see changing or challenging conditions as threats to avoid. This mindset is reactive rather than proactive, lacking in resilience, and less open to learning or collaborating with others.

Ironically, self-protection can make things worse, because over-attention to threats leads to missed opportunities for growth and development.

Why adaptive mindset matters so much

Leaders who model adaptive mindset and behaviours have a clear advantage in turbulence because they build teams and cultures that respond positively to challenge and change. Research has proved this time and again. Instead of being overwhelmed by threats and difficulties, they see and go towards opportunities for achievement, development and partnering with others. They tend to be less stressed, get more satisfaction from their work and reap the benefits of better relationships.

Melbourne Lord Mayor Sally Capp points to a favourite aphorism from Edward Hale that perfectly illustrates adaptive mindset: 'I am only one, but I am one. I cannot do everything, but I can do something.' She holds this observation close, as a personal tool to use in tough conditions. 'It reminds me there's always something within your power that you can do that creates positive momentum.'

An adaptive mindset suits turbulence; a defensive mindset is antagonistic towards it.

Working model adaptive mindset

This model provides a quick reference guide to characteristic ways of thinking and behaving with an adaptive mindset and its opposite, a defensive mindset.

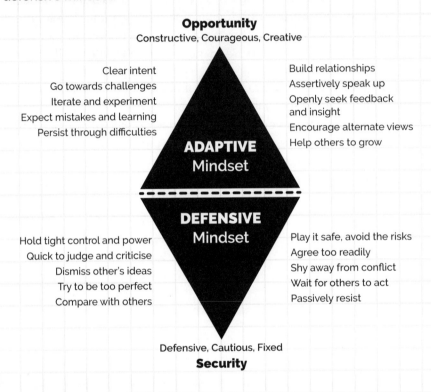

Opportunity
Constructive, Courageous, Creative

Clear intent
Go towards challenges
Iterate and experiment
Expect mistakes and learning
Persist through difficulties

Build relationships
Assertively speak up
Openly seek feedback and insight
Encourage alternate views
Help others to grow

ADAPTIVE
Mindset

DEFENSIVE
Mindset

Hold tight control and power
Quick to judge and criticise
Dismiss other's ideas
Try to be too perfect
Compare with others

Play it safe, avoid the risks
Agree too readily
Shy away from conflict
Wait for others to act
Passively resist

Defensive, Cautious, Fixed
Security

INSTRUCTIONS

Make a physical copy of the model and keep it handy to refer to regularly. It will be useful as a guide for the tools and activities that follow.

The simplest way to use this as a tool is, whenever you feel challenged, to ask yourself three questions:

» Where am I on this model (above or below the midline)?

» What are the costs or benefits of my current mindset?

» What can I do to move my thinking towards opportunities?

Train your adaptive mindset

Whatever disruptions you face as a leader, the premise underpinning the original military thinking about VUCA is 100 per cent right: *a world with greater volatility, uncertainty, complexity and ambiguity (turbulence) requires a different mindset.*

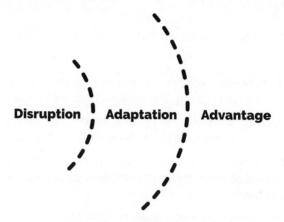

Disruption   **Adaptation**   **Advantage**

Tanya Monro reminds us of the 'why' behind prioritising an adaptive mindset for herself and in the training of leaders across Defence Science and Technology Group. 'This is the chance to make those lurching leaps forward. To make more impact and recast, reposition and organise for that impact.'

The challenges are unquestionably adaptive and so must be the mindset to tackle them, as Andrew McConville reinforces: 'There is a pathway through turbulence, and leaders play the crucial role to support and coach their people and teams to emerge stronger and more resilient.'

The superpower on that pathway is adaptive mindset, so let's get into the primary tool *Mindset awareness training.*

Mindset awareness training

The purpose of this tool is to boost awareness of your protective and defensive responses to threats, and to reorient towards an adaptive mindset. To guide the thought process we use the Mindset Training Canvas.

The following pages examine the three sub-canvases, *See – Squirm – Seek*.

> » **See** is about being aware of when and how challenges trigger your protective and defensive thinking and behaviour.

> » **Squirm** is understanding the natural threat response, and welcoming and embracing it as the sign to switch on.

> » **Seek** is the action you take to go towards the challenge, address it and then decompartmentalise so you release the inevitable stress.

Allocate time to reflect on each step so you lay the foundation for habits that will stick in high-demand situations.

Mindset Training Canvas

See
Threats are inevitable,
self-protection isn't.

1 What's happening ...

2 How do you know ...

Squirm
Welcome threats as natural;
embrace the squirm

3 Welcome to the squirm ...

4 Embrace the squirm ...

Seek
Mindset can change; go towards the
fire ... then decompartmentalise

5 Go towards the fire ...

6 Decompartmentalise after ...

See

It isn't easy or even natural to adopt an adaptive mindset, because humans tend to lean first towards security rather than opportunity. However, adaptive mindset can be trained and strengthened to become your superpower and a great source of advantage in high-demand situations.

The threat response

In 1943 Abraham Maslow published *A Theory of Human Motivation,* whose central idea was that as humans we first seek to meet our basic needs, such as for food, shelter and security, before being motivated towards higher-order needs, such as our social needs, esteem needs and ultimately self-actualisation.

Put simply, you are wired to prioritise protecting yourself from unpleasant and undesirable threats to your survival and safety, above social and self-esteem needs. If these basic needs are met, then you're more likely to flip your thinking towards a mindset of unlocking opportunities for your talents, relationships and community.

It is perfectly normal and expected that work and related stressors will, from time to time, put you on edge, hijack your attention, fragment your thinking and muddy your communication. This is your very natural *threat response*, and anyone trained to operate in high-demand environments is aware of it and even embraces it, because they have the tools to minimise its damaging effects and the ability to turn it into an advantage.

Captain Kevin Sullivan, a trained US Navy pilot, experienced in taking off and landing on the pitching deck of an aircraft carrier at night, is one of those people. He generously shared the graphic experience of his extreme threat response on board Qantas QF72 in 2008.

'The plane is out of control. It's violent and I have to try to regain control, but I also have to communicate with my second officer because we're both getting the fight or flight response. You get tunnel vision, you stop breathing, the blood disappears from your extremities. We have to adapt. I fight myself down to a point where I can think. Breathe. Get some oxygen in the system. And then compartmentalise.'

This is an extreme threat response, but threats of any kind trigger a self-protective or defensive mindset that can make you less effective in complex environments. That's why the first step on the Mindset Training Canvas is to be aware of what's happening.

What is happening?

The first step in becoming aware of how your defensive mindset gets triggered is being alert to potentially challenging situations. Here are examples others have identified:

Presenting on a controversial topic	Realising you made a big error	Dealing with a difficult colleague
Receiving negative feedback	Uncertainty about job security	Handling a crisis situation
Facing a very tight deadline	Experiencing a conflict of values	An overwhelming workload

Turbulence creates its own wake for individuals and teams. SafetyCulture's Chief People Officer, Anna Wenngren, reflects on the realities of the tech sector: 'You have a certain amount of runway and if you can't raise capital you see the end of that runway. So that creates incredible pressure.'

REFLECT
Awareness of defensive mindset

Use the previous examples to help spot situations that might trigger defensiveness.

» Can you think of three to five situations?

» What happens that causes you to think you might be defensive?

» What would you like to do differently?

How do you know?

Tuning in to the telltale signs of your threat response and how it is triggered is the next step in discovering what happens to your mindset in challenging situations. Those signs are underpinned by the motives identified in figure 4.1 and show up in your thinking, feelings and behaviour.

It's a form of mindfulness. Don't judge yourself, just be aware of your very normal feelings and emotions when plans go awry, or crises emerge from nowhere.

Threats and defensiveness are inevitable, but by better understanding your own threat response you can diminish and defuse your protective and defensive thinking and behaviour.

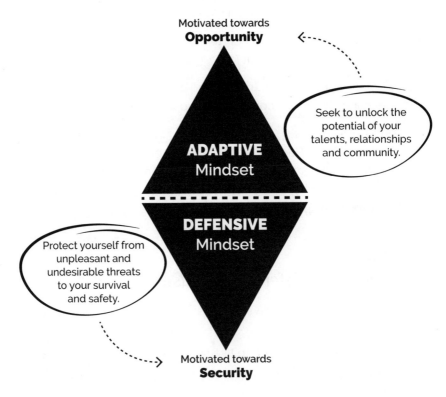

Motivated towards
Opportunity

Seek to unlock the potential of your talents, relationships and community.

ADAPTIVE
Mindset

DEFENSIVE
Mindset

Protect yourself from unpleasant and undesirable threats to your survival and safety.

Motivated towards
Security

Figure 4.1: mindset motives

THINKING AND FEELING

Feelings are the early-warning signs of protective thinking and behaviour, so the more familiar you are with those feelings (and the associated thoughts), the sooner you can spot the signs of defensiveness and apply the tools you'll learn to move towards an adaptive mindset.

REFLECT
Notice your feelings

Choose one of the situations you identified in the previous exercise, where you had an experience of being more protective and defensive than you would have liked. Reflect on the following questions:

How did you think and feel?	Where in your body did you feel it?
Examples:	Examples:
» Muscle tension	» Neck and shoulders
» Anxious and uptight	» Stomach and throat
» Overwhelmed	» Heart rate

BEHAVIOUR

Spotting your own defensive behaviour can be a bit more difficult than noticing feelings, because often we aren't aware of our own protective behaviours, or we view them as warranted and even effective. There are, however, some revealing signs, which are highlighted in the following exercise.

REFLECT
Notice your behaviour

Continue reflecting on situations where you are defensive, and this time focus on behaviours.

Can you spot the signs of defensiveness?

» Over-explaining/justifying
» Blaming/being the victim
» Over-polishing the details
» Resisting by being right/dismissing others
» Counterattacking
» Other

When and how did these signs emerge?

How do you know they are defensive?

Notice how some of the behaviours are about being passive and avoiding, while others are more aggressive or controlling.

Squirm

Squirm

3 **Welcome to the squirm ...**

4 **Embrace the squirm ...**

The next two steps are to recognise and welcome the 'why' behind the emotional squirm, then to embrace it and respond constructively.

Welcome to the squirm

Jump ahead 60 years from Maslow's breakthrough work to 2009, when NeuroLeadership Institute founder David Rock introduced his now widely acclaimed SCARF model, which explained how we are wired to react to social loss with the same threat response as happens when basics like food and shelter are at risk.

Threat and reward

That means the protective mindset (threat response) we've inherited to deal with tigers, snakes and other predators is also triggered by the social experiences we encounter every day in the workplace.

Rock's handy SCARF model highlights five types of threats:

Status	Importance relative to others
Certainty	Being able to predict the future
Autonomy	Sense of control over events
Relatedness	Sense of belonging with others
Fairness	View of fair exchanges

After making the case for a protective mindset, Rock highlighted that threat isn't a one-way street. For example, you might see loss of autonomy as a threat and try to hang on to control, but you might also be motivated by greater autonomy.

One of the keys to navigating turbulence is to welcome the emotional squirm as a natural response. Let's unpack some of that experience.

REFLECT
Unpack the squirm

Consider one or more situations where you have felt threatened, and unpack what might be triggering *your* defensive feelings and behaviours. Following are some questions and prompts to help you do that. As you reflect, take your time, be honest with yourself and don't be surprised if you feel the squirm.

What is triggering the threat and why?

Examples:

» Uncertainty about being expected to make decisions without all the data you crave

» Being excluded from prioritisation conversations

» Unplanned change

What is holding you back or making you less constructive?

What's the worst thing that could happen if you went towards this challenge and engaged with the risk?

Embrace the squirm

Now that you are more aware of what might be triggering your defensive behaviour, it's time to 'embrace the squirm', which means rather than being driven by defensive thinking (avoiding or controlling), you learn to accept and sit with the discomfort as you consider your choices.

Martin describes his initial inner experience of the first COVID-19 threat:

As Graham facilitated a conversation with my team he had aptly titled 'Going towards the fire', I had to pause for a few moments to unpack what was going on in my mind as we confronted the imminent COVID-19 lockdowns. There were flashes of concern about my family, about the disruption of my own plans, snapshots of scenarios where

I was failing my people, being humiliated in public and being the leader who failed the university.

In those early moments of COVID-19, and in many tough moments that followed, I have paused, embraced the squirm and unpacked my very genuine and expected feelings of threat and self-protection. Only then did I turn towards the challenge and use my coping tools, my toolkit for turbulence, to bring an adaptive mindset to the challenges at hand.

REFLECT
Embrace the squirm

Use Martin's example to reflect on what 'embrace the squirm' will mean for you.

» What situations or experiences make you feel uncomfortable, uneasy or fearful?

» How do you typically respond to these feelings? Do you tend to avoid them or confront them?

» How might embracing the squirm benefit you?

» What new opportunities might open up, if you are willing to embrace uncertainty and discomfort?

Seek

How did Kevin Sullivan shift from an extreme threat response to a constructive adaptive mindset in the moments needed to save QF72? When asked, he smiles: 'I had my toolbox.' He explains, 'Navy pilots are expert compartmentalisers so that's what I had to do. Focus on what needed to be done and be innovative, because this hadn't happened before.' He adds, 'Until I had the time to open up those compartments and deal with what was in there.'

Seek

5 Go towards the fire ...

6 Decompartmentalise after ...

Go towards the fire

Going towards challenges, or 'going towards the fire', means taking a courageous and proactive approach to difficulties, rather than avoiding or denying them. It is proactively seeking out challenges, and being willing to confront them head-on, even when uncomfortable or painful.

It's doing what Sally Capp did by publicly admitting 'I got it wrong', and Andrew Westacott did as he confronted the world's media to straight-talk the situation.

Facing into conflict is a great example of going towards the fire. It's about having the difficult conversations and addressing conflicts, not avoiding them. It requires courage and nuance: to be open, to listen, understand and find common ground with others while facing into the disagreement.

Another example is saying 'No' when pressured to say 'Yes'. That is knowing your boundaries and prioritising your own needs, even when that may be unpopular or uncomfortable. It requires assertiveness and holding your power through difficulty. As Tanya Monro puts it, 'Give yourself permission to realise that sometimes less is more.'

Staying composed in a crisis is yet another example of going towards the fire. It's about keeping a clear head and making rational decisions in high-demand situations. It's a mindset of taking charge and leading others, even when there is chaos or uncertainty.

Going towards the fire is a key strategy for personal growth because it boosts resilience and confidence. Being deliberate in choosing this pathway is also a great way to strengthen your problem-solving skills and your ability to navigate difficult situations with poise.

REFLECT
Go towards the fire

Can you recall a situation where you wish you had gone 'towards the fire'? Use the following questions to explore your thoughts and feelings.

What was holding you back or making you less constructive?

Any of these:

» Uncertainty

» Uncomfortable conflict

» Fear of being overwhelmed

» Anxiety about the outcome

» Risk of reputation damage

What were you assuming about the threats or risks in this situation?

Are those assumptions 100 per cent right, or did you have some wriggle room to perhaps challenge them?

What would one of those assumptions look like if you reframed it towards opportunity?

Decompartmentalise after

Taking time to decompartmentalise after an emotionally challenging experience is essential for wellbeing and for future growth.

In extreme situations the impacts of unresolved emotions and other issues can have long-term negative effects on mental health. Unpacking the experience is important to gain insight into your thoughts, feelings and behaviours, and to develop a better understanding of yourself and your reactions to similar situations in the future.

REFLECT
Decompartmentalise after

Whenever you have an experience that shakes you a little or a lot, it is wise to debrief with a few reflective questions and a wise colleague or professional. This frame is a starting guide:

1. Event	2. Emotions
» What was the event or experience?	» What emotions did you experience?
» Describe it in detail.	» How intense were they?
3. Thoughts	**4. Strategies**
» What thoughts arose during this experience?	» What coping strategies did you employ?
» Which were helpful or unhelpful?	» What worked well and what have you learned for the future?

Recap

Your performance in a challenging situation is always going to be determined by your own 'inner game'. As for an elite athlete, the key to winning that game is your mindset (attitude, beliefs).

It is natural to view some of these situations as threats and to feel anxious or frustrated about uncertainty, loss of control, interpersonal conflict and damage to reputation. The risk is that you get pulled into a defensive mindset where instead of proactively seeking opportunity you act to overly protect yourself.

That protection can be subtle, like avoiding action and staying in a 'holding pattern', or it can be more overt and show up in poor communication and decision making.

Don't underestimate the power of just being aware of how your protective behaviours can unintentionally hold back progress towards your goals. Repeat the steps on the Mindset Training Canvas whenever you experience unhelpful defensiveness. With practice you will strengthen your ability to flip towards an adaptive mindset in the moment.

The activities you have just completed focused on your own mindset. Now let's turn to a few thoughts on the challenge of shifting mindsets at scale across your team or organisation.

Mindset can change at scale

Is it possible to make adaptive change stick in turbulent conditions?

The history of workplace change management is awash with statistics suggesting alarming failure rates, and personal change isn't much different. Even when confronted with graphic personal imperatives, such as changing lifestyle habits after a heart attack, the numbers are little or no better.

Nevertheless, under the right conditions adaptive change happens, and it doesn't take anywhere near as long as the doomsayers might suggest.

Why change doesn't have to be slow

If you'd been a bank customer in Australia in 1974 you wouldn't have had a credit card, and chances are your attitude towards those plastic cards would have been cautious at best.

Despite those prevailing attitudes several banks decided to come together to launch Australia's first homegrown credit card (Diners Club and American Express cards were in use for specific retailers). They knew the uptake would likely be slow, however, because credit cards were viewed as risky and a good way to get into debt. The banks relied on cognitive dissonance to achieve an astounding outcome. Here's how they did it.

They mailed out the plastic cards, along with encouraging messages, and included a $300 credit limit on suitable accounts, alongside a marketing campaign. Then they waited. Soon people started using the cards, even those who said they wouldn't. Why? Because it was convenient, particularly when they found themselves without cash and wanted something (there were no ATMs and banks had very limited business hours). This created a state of dissonance or, in other words, a misfit between mindset ('Don't use these risky credit cards') and behaviours ('I just used the credit card').

Humans hate dissonance so they had two options: cut up the card and call it a minor slip-up, or keep the card and change the attitude. The results speak for themselves: over a million cardholders within 18 months. What happened? Attitudes shifted to match the behaviour: 'I can use a credit card responsibly to make handy purchases while keeping any debt under control.' Change in mindset and habits can and does happen at scale and pace.

Not convinced? Try another example, like working from home in COVID-19, or even just attending online meetings. In just one month in 2020, the leaders of organisations who expected their people to show up for work, and considered online meetings a poor substitute for the 'real thing', embraced new ways of working — literally overnight.

Paul Duldig smiles while recounting an IT team meeting at the Australian National University just before COVID-19: 'It went something like, "We've just implemented Microsoft 365 online and paid for a licence. There's this thing called Teams and we're not sure what it is, but we've got it for free, alongside SharePoint. It will need a big change management budget and engagement right across the university will take time, maybe three years." Two months later everyone knew how to use Teams and SharePoint!'

Change in mindset and habits can and does happen at scale and pace.

People change when their underlying assumptions change. Old assumptions, such as *credit cards are risky, online meetings don't work* and *you can't trust people to work from home*, hold the old behaviours in place until something else comes along and we flip, and that flip happens fastest when we make the implicit explicit.

Make the implicit explicit

Here we turn to Chief Defence Scientist Tanya Monro, who relentlessly coaches her leaders and teams to be aware of their mindset and move from defensive to adaptive by developing the habits and capabilities to 'make the implicit explicit'.

Defence Science and Technology Group (DSTG) had historically operated in a 'linear' environment, with clear boundaries between divisions and the domains of the defence force and associated big defence companies and universities. The recent significant shifts in geopolitics and technology (including the AUKUS alliance) transformed that environment almost overnight into an open ecosystem. In response, Tanya and her leadership team initiated a new operating model. The new model challenged and changed many of the core assumptions about the role of DSTG and subsequently the role of their operating units and people. The intent of the new operating model is summarised in the DSTG strategy 'More Together' and is designed to equip them to perform effectively in turbulence that will likely continue for some time.

'Making the implicit explicit starts with people naming what they are having to deal with and tabling the assumptions they carry with them,' Tanya explains. 'It is shifting from the habit of defending to a much more open and constructive style. When things aren't explicit people hold their own interpretation and assumptions. That can play out in second guessing the motivations of others or reacting defensively when decisions are made that impact your area.'

Throughout the book we ask you to 'make the implicit explicit' because it opens up conversations to opportunities and is a powerful way to drive change at scale.

Learnings

» An **adaptive mindset** equips you and your team to deal with fast and unpredictable change, navigate through uncertainty, collaborate on complex entangled problems, and embrace ambiguity and paradoxes.

» A **defensive mindset** can hold you back, because it reinforces a cautious and fixed approach and treats changing or challenging conditions as threats to avoid.

» **Threats and defensiveness** are inevitable; however, you can understand, reduce and/or defuse your defensive thinking and behaviour.

» You can train your adaptive mindset to become a great source of advantage in high-demand situations. The **Mindset Training Canvas** provides the framework and steps to train your adaptive mindset.

» Accept your threat reaction as natural and be alert to **what's really holding you back**.

» Mindset can change rapidly when the assumptions shift **from implicit to explicit** and you **go towards the fire**.

» Reduce the pull of your protective mindset to act in ways that better suit turbulent conditions, and be sure to take time to **decompartmentalise** after particularly challenging experiences.

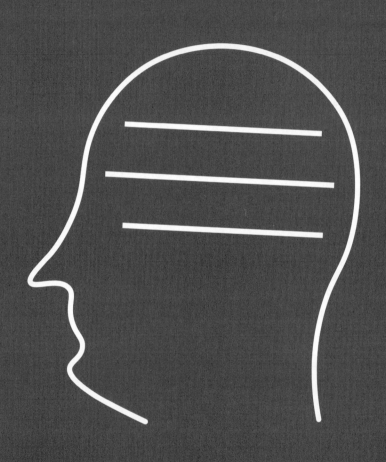

3

Recalibrate

... your leadership paradigms

In Part 2 you learned about linear and **nonlinear challenges** and the power of an **adaptive mindset** for navigating change and turbulence. In this part you will start by exploring the idea of paradigms as an essential aspect of mindset. From there you step through **four 'recalibrations'** that are common among advantage leaders. Those recalibrations address **values**, **change**, **pace** and **self-care**. You will evaluate your own mindset and mental models at each step and add to your toolkit for turbulence.

CHAPTER 5
Paradigm shifts

What are paradigms, and why do they matter? How do you adapt when a paradigm shift upends your world? What about getting ahead of the game to create your own paradigm shifts?

When people think of the aged care industry, most picture the care homes and villages spreading rapidly across the country. Care Connect, a not for profit established in 1994, operates to a different paradigm: in-home care.

One of Australia's largest providers, Care Connect has supported more than 85000 Australians to live independently at home and stay connected to their community.

After a decade at the helm of Care Connect, Chief Executive Paul Ostrowski knows a bit about paradigms, because his organisation's core purpose not only challenges the still dominant residential care paradigm but also puts Care Connect at the leading edge of the shift from traditional models (where healthcare professionals dictate care plans) to putting the person in charge of their own plans.

When asked about paradigm shifts, Paul immediately separates the conversation into two types: responsive and proactive.

» **Responsive** shifts saw him and his team respond and adapt to two big events: the Royal Commission into Aged Care with its subsequent transformation of funding models, governance and care frameworks, and the COVID-19 pandemic with its immediate and continuing impacts.

   »   **Proactive** shifts meant Care Connect challenged and reinvented its own thinking and practices, starting with the core business model of in-home care then extending into aspects such as their innovative multi-service coordination system.

Paul observes, 'The aged care environment continues to be extremely turbulent. COVID is still a very real risk because we're dealing with a vulnerable client cohort; there are enormous funding challenges; acute workforce shortages exacerbated by the spluttering restart of migration; and a workforce exhausted by the COVID response, and yet there's still a job to be done.'

Looking forward, Paul demonstrates the adaptive mindset of an advantage leader: 'We have to be nimble to adapt to the change and transformation coming at us, but we also have to be proactive and shape our own future.'

This ability to navigate the disruption of paradigm shifts and at the same time to be the initiator of innovation is fundamental to leading through turbulence.

Paradigms and mindsets

Paradigms are powerful and are another example of mental models through which we see and interpret the world, which raises the question of the distinction between *mindset* and *paradigm*.

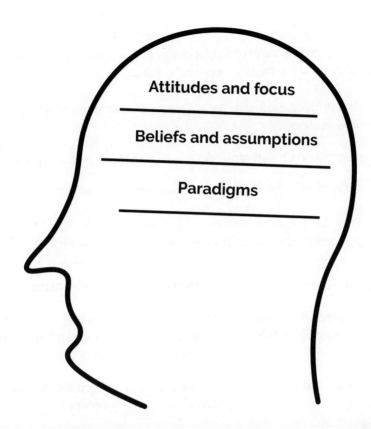

There are different views on this; however, we use mindset as encompassing paradigms, beliefs, assumptions, attitudes and focus, because they are all part of the mix that makes up your adaptive mindset, which, as you know, is essential to navigating through turbulence.

A *paradigm shift*, according to Thomas Kuhn, is 'like wearing inverted lenses'—in other words, flipping things upside down. Such a shift is triggered by the 'aha' moment of insight when we suddenly understand something in a completely different way.

Business students learn about paradigm shifts through case studies on digital cameras, video streaming, smartphones, hybrid working, chatbots and the like.

Turbulence often renders current paradigms obsolete, while opening the pathway to new ways of thinking and doing. Advantage leaders like Paul Ostrowski seize these opportunities to be:

»   alert and *responsive* to paradigm shifts that affect their organisations

»   *proactive* in challenging and innovating through those paradigms

»   open to *recalibrating* their own leadership paradigms.

Let's address these three elements by exploring the topics illustrated in figure 5.1 (recalibrating is covered in the following chapters).

	A. Responsive	**B. Proactive**	**C. Recalibrating**
	Alert and responsive to paradigm shifts	*Proactive in challenging and innovating*	*Open to recalibrating your own leadership paradigms*
	'Ride the storm'	**'Create the storm'**	**'Recalibrate your mindset'**
1	Understand your new context	Scan for opportunities	Anchor on personal values
2	Reimagine your strategy	Challenge and change assumptions	Let go and accept the externality of change
3	Switch on your team	Get your team on board	Dial up the learning
4	10x communication	Coach for innovation	Prioritise self-care
5	Loop and learn	Nail the landing	Be the coach your people need

Figure 5.1: leading the way on paradigm shifts

Element A. Ride the storm

Australian-based software company SafetyCulture is recognised as among Australia's most innovative companies and has been shaking paradigms around managing workforce safety and quality since 2004.

When asked about the impact of the pandemic and other turbulence, Chief People Officer Anna Wenngren observes, 'From the perspective of business turbulence COVID-19 was nothing compared with the capital crunch that hit the whole tech sector in the second half of 2022.'

Anna explains, 'We've gone from an environment where companies had to scale ahead because investment money was flowing, to an incredibly turbulent and volatile environment.'

SafetyCulture made some tough strategic choices that boiled down to one core message, 'Pivot to become profitable', which represented a complete change of company strategy. Anna Wenngren calls it 'riding the storm', and it is a remarkable story of how the leaders of SafetyCulture preserved and strengthened their culture, as was recognised when the company was named as one of Australia's best workplaces in tech in 2023.

We borrow Anna's image of 'riding the storm' to share five core practices you will need to embrace to be an advantage leader who responds constructively to paradigm shifts in your world.

1. Understand your new context

In turbulence context is key, so you must understand the situation and the implications for your business model and your culture. For example, when ChatGPT was first emerging Martin noticed a reluctance on the part of many senior leaders to roll up their sleeves, use the tool and begin to explore the challenges and opportunities it presents for their enterprises. That defensive mindset can put organisations into a dangerously reactive mode.

2. Reimagine your strategy

Paradigm shifts upend strategy, or at the very least can change strategic trajectory in big ways. Brett Wickham is Managing Director of ACCIONA Energia Australia, a fast-growing energy company that develops, builds, owns and operates renewable energy projects. Paradigm change for ACCIONA came when Australia signed the Paris Accords to substantially reduce greenhouse emissions. That meant an almost overnight flip in the renewable energy industry from famine to feast. Brett observes, 'We literally cannot run fast enough and cannot grow fast enough. We've got the physical challenges of taking what was a boutique business three years ago with 50 staff and will become 300 and growing at the end of the year.'

It's important to run scenarios and contingency plans alongside your day-to-day delivery. This is what Martin calls 'leapfrogging': focusing on the immediate issues and on the next horizon at the same time. That requires excellent partnering and teamwork among leaders and teams at all levels of an enterprise.

3. Switch on your team

Of course, your team must always be engaged, but sometimes you need to flick the switch to ensure everyone is working together as one team to adapt to the change. This is particularly important when there is a fast-moving paradigm shift and there is no time to be stuck in what Dobbs and associates called the 'tyranny of conventional wisdom'. SEEK Chief Financial Officer Kate Koch offers an idea: 'I keep saying to my team, "Let's just do a few different scenarios." Because I think it's all about scenario planning. Sometimes it might be nothing or something significant, but it stimulates the thinking and the conversations, which makes us more adaptable.'

4. 10x communication

Sally Capp sums up the need to ramp up communication: 'The whole communications paradigm is different. The way we use, communicate and distribute information, the relationships we've got to build. All the expectations are higher and harder, and we must respond to that.' When in doubt and sensing or seeing paradigm shifts, the smart move is to ramp up communication in all directions.

5. Loop and learn

Day-to-day leadership of your team requires balancing your attention on people and on the task, on agility and stability, and on the long and short term. It's the business equivalent of *Aviate – Navigate – Communicate*, which we call *Align – Collaborate – Learn*, the continuous cycle of aligning, collaborating and learning with your team to ride through the storm. To help you do just that, chapter 8 addresses the topic of *dialling up the learning* and chapter 13 focuses on *team learning*.

INSIGHT EXERCISE
Ride the storm

Take a few moments to reflect on a recent paradigm shift in your industry, then rate the response of your team, from 1 = Poor to 5 = Excellent.

How effectively did your team ride the storm?	1	2	3	4	5
Understood the new context	O	O	O	O	O
Reimagined the strategy	O	O	O	O	O
Switched on as a team	O	O	O	O	O
10x communication	O	O	O	O	O
Looped and learned	O	O	O	O	O

Element B. Create the storm

In his ground-breaking book *Paradigms*, Joel Barker offered the insight that new paradigms inevitably arise from the problems that the current paradigm doesn't solve. This sounds somewhat obvious, but what does it really mean?

Firstly, it explains why suitcases have wheels, how Uber so quickly disrupted the taxi industry, and how smartphones gobbled up GPS navigation, cameras and music players. Each of these new paradigms solved the problems of earlier paradigms.

Secondly, to move from responding to creating your own paradigm shifts, you must know where to look and be alert to the challenges that often beset the champions of such change.

We call this 'Create the storm'.

1. Scan for opportunities

Problems with your current paradigms is the first place to look for opportunities to challenge and change paradigms. That might sound easy but it's not. Why? Because when you start pointing out faults with a technology, or a product or service, or the organisation design, or any other aspect of the business, people will likely treat it as criticism. This can often blind them to possibilities, which means resistance needs to be managed deliberately and delicately. Many of the tools for collaboration and decision making, covered in the next part, are designed to help you do that.

2. Challenge and change assumptions

Remember Tanya Monro's advice to make the implicit explicit by encouraging and coaching people to name their assumptions? How do you do that? By asking questions of yourself and others:

> » What do you believe that caused you to form that opinion?

> » How confident are you that your assumptions are accurate or true?

> » What alternative explanations might challenge your assumptions?

Asked about changed assumptions, Sally Capp observes, 'Operating in certainty is gone. I look back and realise how much certainty we had, how much we just took for granted. We could take so many shortcuts in our day based on assumptions on how things will work, and a lot of those assumptions have gone out the window.'

In the spirit of advantage leadership she confirms, 'We're trying to turn that into a positive; get to know people better, understand how our products can be better, our service better. It's a complete rethink.'

By creating a culture where assumptions are surfaced and challenged, you greatly increase the likelihood of new paradigms arising.

3. Get your team on board

New paradigms must be incubated and tested in the real world to have any chance of success. This requires a 'one team' commitment to embracing change even though it can be uncomfortable and awkward. Kate Koch offers a hint: 'Telling the team what isn't going to change can be as helpful as telling them what will.' In the next part you will be introduced to a host of tools designed specifically to help you to align your team and boost collaboration and co-creation to ensure innovation happens at pace.

4. Coach for innovation

Turbulence can be exhausting, and driving innovation requires energy and freshness. The Royal Children's Hospital Melbourne CEO Bernadette McDonald noticed the prevailing narrative about fatigue and was wary it could be counterproductive. She set out to change the conversations with a new call to action: 'Let's talk about the future and what's going to be different.' From that simple start, a wave of momentum built for a transformation of the vision and values of the hospital.

5. Nail the landing

How will you know if your new paradigm is successful? It requires clear metrics and a willingness to be open to feedback in all its forms and to constantly learn and adjust strategy. That's why you are building your toolkit for turbulence. In chapter 13 you'll find an interesting model called *Sky to Ground*, which helps shape the mindset needed to nail the landing.

INSIGHT EXERCISE
Create the storm

Take a few moments to reflect on the extent to which you and your team have been proactive in shaping the paradigms. Rate from 1 = Poor to 5 = Excellent.

How effectively are you creating the storm?	1	2	3	4	5
Scanning for opportunities	O	O	O	O	O
Challenging and changing assumptions	O	O	O	O	O
Getting the team on board	O	O	O	O	O
Coaching for innovation	O	O	O	O	O
Nailing the landing	O	O	O	O	O

Element C. Recalibrate your mindset

We can't predict whether hybrid working is here to stay, if the four-day work week will become a thing or how generative AI will disrupt the very nature of how we work. We are confident, however, that the paradigm shifts of recent years will create permanent disruption and that disruption will give birth to more paradigm shifts.

Everyone we have spoken with while researching this book shares the observation of Chris Tanti, Leukemia Foundation's CEO: 'You can predict it's going to be unpredictable.'

With that in mind, we sorted through the conversations with advantage leaders to answer one fundamental question: *What are the most important mindset recalibrations that advantage leaders need to make?*

Five themes emerged consistently and in a language that hints at the intention of each:

1. Anchor on personal values.

2. Let go. Accept the externality of change.

3. Dial up the learning.

4. Prioritise self-care.

5. Be the coach your people need.

The next four chapters will explore the first four of these themes in detail, including tools and techniques you can use for yourself and your team to turn adversity to advantage. The fifth topic, *Be the coach your people need*, is covered in chapter 14.

Learnings

» Paradigm shifts are the 'aha' **moments of insight** when we suddenly understand something in a completely different way.

» Turbulence often makes current paradigms **obsolete**, while opening the pathway to new ways of thinking and doing.

» To live, work and lead in a turbulent environment, it is equally important to:

  » be **responsive** to transformation in the external environment

  » **proactively** reshape paradigms affecting your organisation

  » continually **recalibrate** your own leadership paradigms.

» The ability to **navigate** the disruption of paradigm shifts and at the same time to be the **initiator of innovation** is fundamental to leading through turbulence.

CHAPTER 6

It starts with you. Anchor on personal values

How do you make decisions when all the usual guideposts have gone? If there is no 'right decision', then what is the right decision? How do advantage leaders make good decisions under extreme uncertainty?

Reimagine

Despite their apparent slowness, the World Health Organization became the 'lead domino' when, on March 11th, 2020, the outbreak of COVID-19 was declared a global pandemic. That changed the psychology and decision making of governments worldwide, ushering in extreme measures. Italy was the epicentre, with thousands of reported illnesses and deaths. Australia closed its borders to all non-residents and non-citizens on the 20th. By the 23rd the Dow Jones Industrial Average closed down almost 40 per cent on the previous month. A day later India went into national lockdown with only four hours' notice. Millions of people were stranded without access to food, shelter or transportation. Decisions were being made in the extreme uncertainty and ambiguity of a 'black swan event' (a term popularised by Nassim Nicholas Taleb in his book of the same name to describe rare and seemingly unpredictable events that have severe and potentially catastrophic consequences).

Within a few weeks of the onset of Melbourne's COVID-19 lockdowns it became clear that RMIT University, like all Australian universities, was facing unparalleled financial and operational challenges. The severity of the situation meant confronting the imperative to reduce expenditure by more than $300 million.

There was no playbook, no guidelines, only a clear viability target and a world of pain.

Graham Winter: black swan decisions

Amongst the turmoil and uncertainty of the early days of the pandemic Martin moved quickly to establish Project Reimagine: a complete rethink of the way the university operated. It would be vastly different from plans decided pre-COVID and a world away from the continuing growth, innovation and opportunity people had been expecting.

Martin knew the time would soon come when he would be called upon to make impossibly difficult decisions about people and programs he had nurtured and cared for dearly. Knowing him, these would be decisions he'd take very personally. He needed new tools.

Over my career I have observed top sports coaches who every year face the challenge to cut from their roster players who had been integral to the team and almost like family. It is gut-wrenching, but they do it year on year, and those ex-players love them for the way they do it and the culture they create.

Every one of these coaches exemplifies authenticity. They never hide behind a process, a rule, even a team value or principle. They lean into these situations, sometimes openly shedding tears, always heartbroken to take away something that those dear to them care about. They go to this challenge 100 per cent human.

So this was a conversation Martin and I had to have, because part of my role was to equip and support Martin to make the best *black swan decisions*.

Accompanying the conversation, this is what I wrote to him.

> *Martin, I'm asking you to reflect on your deepest, strongest personal values. The values that when all clarity and certainty are*

stripped away, you can turn to and use to guide the decisions you make for yourself, your team and the whole community relying on your leadership.

Take as much time as you need. Think back through your early years. Speak to those closest to you and when you're ready, come back to me with the two or three values you are ready to anchor on no matter what happens.

When you've found those values, it's time to sit with your team and tell your story.

Help them to understand what these values mean to you at an emotional level. Be vulnerable. Make sure they know that these are your true north.

They will follow you.

Real values aren't on the wall

Enterprise values are extremely important in framing and shaping organisation culture. When leading in turbulent conditions, however, it is personal values that can be one of the greatest assets to guide you and others through volatility, uncertainty, complexity and ambiguity.

It wasn't Qantas values that guided Captain Kevin Sullivan to forgo the expected announcement from the flight deck and instead choose to walk the whole length of the plane and back, speaking to passengers and crew, in a cabin with holes in the ceiling covered in bits of scalp and blood, and with people moaning and crying. 'I'm in charge. I'm still in command. I must lead,' he says solemnly. He'd landed on a 10 000-foot runway of an airport with no facilities for immediate support. 'I'm not going to hide on the flight deck. It's confronting, but I know what I must do. They've been through hell. I must be seen. I must be strong. I must show compassion, and I need to give them an explanation of what happened, even though I don't *know* what happened.'

Anchoring on personal values gives you three huge advantages when facing into high-pressure, time-dependent decisions.

Value 1	Value 2	Value 3
Authenticity	*Awareness*	*Adaptability*
No facade	Alert to biases	Freed from linear rules

1. Authenticity

The last thing you need when feeling pressured is to put up a facade or apply some artificial framework to make decisions. You must show up as your authentic best self; it takes enough cognitive load to handle challenges without the added pressure of playing a role. You owe that to yourself and your people. Leading through values, anchored deeply in your life experiences, will mean you can be straight with how and why you make decisions in times of adversity. Kate Koch: 'Being a distant leader is a thing of the past.'

2. Awareness

Societal norms around environment, gender, sexuality, race and the like are being challenged, contested and changed almost daily. This can make it difficult to be open on the one hand, and yet clear on your 'moral compass' on the other. Anchoring on values and principles will help you to be more aware of your own beliefs and cultural conditioning in this complex and evolving context, and to be more understanding of others in your team and enterprise.

3. Adaptability

Clarity of values and principles will help you (and potentially your team) to avoid being bound by rules and bureaucratic process unsuited for fluid environments. Personal and organisational values and the associated principles enhance adaptability by providing a framework for effective decision making and setting the tone of conversations about purpose and priorities, which are powerful tools to align teams and whole enterprises.

Former Group CEO of Asahi Beverages Oceania Region Robert Iervasi shares a strong framework anchored on values, principles and purpose: 'It gives you clarity on why the organisation exists, which is to protect our people and the community and serve the needs of your customers and consumers, and nothing else. It quickly enables you to decide what activity could be stopped and eliminated for a period of time, and ensure all of the hierarchies are across it and endorse it.'

CORE VALUES

With those three advantages in mind, and under great pressure and urgency, Martin reflected, debated, decided and anchored on his values.

Three times we discussed the values and three times he went back to have deeper conversations with people who knew him well and cared about him enough to give him their unvarnished truth.

He landed on three core values: *courage*, *care* and *mateship*.

To give you a sense of how this exercise is deeply personal, here is an introduction from Graham, then a snapshot of how Martin explained why he chose *courage*, what it means to him and why he falls back on the principles underlying this value whenever a difficult decision is required.

Graham Winter: on meeting Martin for the first time

I first met Martin on the evening prior to facilitating a meeting of Vice Chancellors. Standing in small groups chatting about the issues of the day I heard him before I saw him, and that's important to know. The group nearest to the entrance grew louder and more animated, and an Australian voice tinged with an American accent cut through. I was facing the other way, but with a quick glance I caught a glimpse of a relatively short, grey-haired man who was greeting the group as you would dear friends not seen for some time. His energy changed the group, and seemed to change the room, as I observed people smiling in his direction.

A few minutes passed before the slightly accented voice approached me from behind and issued a cheeky challenge, 'So *you're* the facilitator.' I spun around to be greeted by a man walking towards me with an unusual gait and offering his left hand backwards to shake hands. His gaze was strong, his handshake firm and his greeting warm. I can honestly say that was the only time in the years I have known Martin that I saw him as someone with a disability.

Martin's words to his team will explain the rest.

Martin Bean: courage is my starting point

Here's what I told my team at the outset of COVID-19.

> When Graham encouraged me to find and share my anchor values with you, I first chose 'courage' because that is the most powerful one for me. I was born with severe scoliosis, which resulted in invasive spinal surgery at age 12. I was also born with partial spasticity on my right side, which means I don't have the balance, strength and movement in the same way most people do. That has presented me with many challenges, particularly as I grew up in a generation nowhere near as understanding and inclusive of people with a disability.
>
> I remember at a very young age being sidelined by the coach of what must have been an under-nine soccer team. The coach, with no medical experience, just decided I should sit on the sideline rather than kick a ball around with other kids.
>
> My good fortune in life was to be surrounded by amazing and caring role models. My mum and others around me were angry and upset. They saw the way I was treated as unfair, and downright wrong.

I don't recall exactly what they said to the coach, but what they said to me was a statement carved into my life: 'There's just no such word as can't, Martin. If you want to do it, and you want it badly enough, we'll figure out a way for you to do it.'

And so, from those early days, and despite the pain and impediment that comes with this condition, whenever I've come up against adversity, my mindset has never been, 'It's insurmountable, it can't be done'. It's always, 'Let's take a look at it. What is it I'm trying to achieve and what is it that I might need to do differently to make it possible?'

The toolkit I have isn't the same as the one others have. But that's the point of a toolkit: you select the tools you have available, the ones that work for you, and you figure out how to get the job done, no matter how long it takes or how hard it might be. So, I guess, deeply ingrained in me is the belief that you've got to be courageous in the face of adversity.

It's actually quite easy to play the game of "No, look, I can't do that," particularly if you've got a demonstrable disability, because nobody's going to push back or hold it against you. But that game plan nearly always results in a suboptimal outcome and over time it erodes self-confidence and self-belief. You're better off trying, and arriving at your own conclusion that you can't, than letting anyone in life decide that for you.

I remember learning to ride a bike — oh, was that a challenge! With the offset balance of my body, I had so many bruises, scrapes and scars from falling off that bike, until one day it clicked, and I figured out how I needed to position my body on a bike to stay upright. I had to capture my own sense of balance rather than everybody else's sense of balance. It's amazing in life how valuable it can be to develop your own sense of balance rather than always following others' view of the 'right' way to do things.

So along came COVID-19, another situation where on the face of it you would say, we can't win at this game. That might be true, but my values are telling me pretty loudly that as long as we're clear about what our goal is, and that we might not tackle it in the same way we usually would, or the way others will do it, we've got this! And you know what, it's really important for our staff and students that we get this done.

And I guess my value of courage is what I bring into the room right now, I'm up for it if you are too.

Courage is my starting point because I refuse simply to put my hands in the air, blame the virus, blame the federal government, blame whoever, and instead I say, 'No, let's be courageous and say we're willing to get the job done and get it done the right way, our way. And if we go down swinging, that's better than not trying at all.'

The values anchor

Personal values, when combined with clarity of purpose, are a tool that becomes your north star when moving from adversity to advantage.

Murray–Darling Basin Authority CEO Andrew McConville reinforces the role of leadership here: 'Rather than trying to remove turbulence altogether, you've got to equip people with the mental and emotional tools to navigate it successfully. That starts with strong alignment with purpose and values. They are the stabilising force during uncertainty.'

Let's find your anchor values by using the primary tool *Anchor on personal values*.

Anchor on personal values

Personal values are the foundation on which to make tough decisions and choices. Identify your core values, then decide if you want to share them with your team.

INSTRUCTIONS

1. Allocate up to two hours in a relaxing or inspiring place.

2. Follow the Guidepoints below which take you through these steps:

    Step 1. Commit to the process

    Step 2. Reflect and explore

    Step 3. Record insights

    Step 4. Choose to share

    Step 5. Apply your values anchor

3. If you decide to share them with your team, then prepare your stories and lean into the experience.

Guidepoints

Follow these steps to guide you through the process of discovering and affirming your anchor values.

Step 1. Commit to the process.

We are asking you to reflect on your deepest, strongest personal values. The values that when all clarity and certainty are stripped away, you can turn to and use to guide the decisions you make for yourself, your team and the whole community relying on your leadership.

Take as much time as you need.

Step 2. Reflect and explore

Think back through your early years. Speak to those closest to you and when you're ready, come back with the two or three values you are ready to anchor on no matter what happens.

Step 3. Record insights

Write a sentence or set of points about each core value to capture its essence and how you apply it to make difficult decisions and choices. Complete a *values frame*, like the following example from Martin, to capture your work.

Martin's values frame		
Courage	**Care**	**Mateship**
No matter how much I would like to avoid confronting an issue such as the performance of a team member whom I care for, life has taught me that being courageous and having the tough conversation is not just the right choice, it's the only choice.	Even when tough decisions need to be made or bad news needs to be shared, I believe you can still care deeply for the individual impacted and treat them with dignity and respect.	When life or work hands you the most difficult of challenges, I'm always at my best when I tackle them with others whom I respect and who I know have my back. Achievement is so much sweeter when shared with others.

Step 4. Choose to share

When you've found those values it's time to decide if you want to sit with your team and tell your story. Help them to understand what these values mean to you at an emotional level. Be vulnerable. Make sure they know that these are your true north.

Step 5. Apply your values anchor

Use your values to guide your decision making in difficult situations.

Values in action

By defining your *anchor values*, you create one of the most important foundations for navigating turbulence because, irrespective of the challenges, you have a tool to help guide your thinking and action.

VCE conversations during COVID-19 often focused on how to take care of staff and students, even when leadership decisions would have a negative impact on their lives. It was a living embodiment of Martin's core values of courage and care.

For Captain Sullivan, the personal cost of experiencing QF72 has been immense. It is heart-warming to hear his response when asked how he reflects on the decisions he made to lead when on the ground in Learmonth: 'I'm very proud of what I did.' And for the 315 passengers and crew it was his personal values in action for which they will be forever grateful.

Learnings

» In the early days of the COVID-19 pandemic there was much ambiguity and uncertainty as borders closed and people went into lockdown. It was a classic **black swan event**.

» Authentic leaders **never hide** behind a process, a rule or even a team value or principle. They lean into situations 100 per cent human.

» When all clarity and certainty are stripped away, turn to your **anchor values** to guide the decisions you make for yourself, your team and all those relying on your leadership.

» Find your anchor values in conversations with people who know you well. Expect this to be an emotional experience, particularly as you **craft your stories**.

» When you are ready, sit with your team and tell your story. Help them to understand what the values mean to you at an emotional level. **Be vulnerable**. Make sure they know that these values are your true north. Your team will follow you.

» Record your thinking on the **values frame**, and refer to it whenever you need guidance in difficult times.

CHAPTER 7

Let go. Accept the externality of change

How do you exercise control in an environment where much is out of your control? What is your current relationship with uncertainty and ambiguity?

How do advantage leaders navigate inevitable loss without being thrown off course?

If you studied psychology in the 1970s you would have learned about Martin Seligman's research into 'learned helplessness', which described how uncontrollable adverse events can make people feel powerless and passive. Significant societal and personal problems such as long-term unemployment, substance abuse, depression and anxiety have been closely linked to this concept.

If you were still studying psychology in the 1990s you might have smiled when Seligman reappeared, this time as a bestselling author with a much less gloomy book title, *Learned Optimism,* and the message that optimism contributes to wellbeing in adults and children.

Optimism is now a cornerstone of the Positive Psychology movement and along with its opposite, pessimism, plays a vital role in building resilience and adaptability.

The psychology of certainty and control

Optimism sounds like an obvious way to approach the world but what if you lose your sense of certainty, of being able to plan, while facing seemingly endless negative events? Why wouldn't you pessimistically assume you have no control over your world and no agency to shape it?

Advantage leaders speak about their sense of having had less control during and following the pandemic. Stay at home, don't drive more than five kilometres, wear a mask, get vaccinated, swipe the QR code — each was a direct challenge to personal autonomy and sense of certainty.

The impacts of the pandemic and what followed — rising energy costs, supply chain shortages, a war for talent, increasing social activism, tightened governance, cyber-attacks, media intrusion, AI and so on — have contributed to the perception (or reality) that leadership control has shifted. Add the increasing rejection by the workforce of overly hierarchical leadership and it is reasonable to expect leaders to feel less control of their environment than pre-pandemic.

How do you maintain a healthy sense of control, confidence and agency that is suited to the shifting norms of a post-pandemic world?

Chris Tanti is CEO of the Leukaemia Foundation, a national not-for-profit organisation dedicated to conquering blood cancers. Appointed during the pandemic, Chris encountered turbulence in many forms, including staff turnover of greater than 50 per cent and a complete change in the Board. He had to guide the organisation through transformation, and all the challenges of caring for and supporting an immuno-compromised community during the pandemic and beyond.

Seeking perspective, Chris reached out to a network of colleagues working in leadership roles across the world. They surprised him. 'They were running hard and trying to control things that were clearly out of their control. You don't have any control on how the market is going to respond, and you don't know what governments are going to do, or whether it's going to get worse before it gets better. The approach we took, and it's still our approach, is, "All we can do is keep our eye on the prize and go with the instability".'

Go with the instability

To follow Chris's advice, we turned to the splendidly named Stockdale Paradox, first brought to public attention by Jim Collins in his iconic book *Good to Great,* in which he described the experience of Admiral James Stockdale, a United States pilot and prisoner of war for seven years in Vietnam.

Now a commonly shared story in leadership development, Stockdale credited his ability to adapt to and survive physical and psychological trauma by adopting a mindset we would describe as a midpoint between 'hopeful optimism' and 'helpless pessimism'.

Prisoners who adopted a hopeful outlook were continually disappointed by events sliding past with no change, while the helpless pessimists were crushed by the sense of no way forward.

hummgroup Group CEO Rebecca James shares the value of a similar approach arising from the company's experience with turbulence: 'One of the learnings for me, and something we've spent a lot of time investing in with our leaders, is to not to be too overly optimistic or hopeful because you set yourself up for shocks or to run out of steam.'

The Stockdale approach was both pragmatic and purposeful. He chose to believe that things would eventually be better, provided he didn't dwell on that. His story shaped one of Collins' best-known admonitions: 'You must confront the most brutal facts of your current reality, whatever they might be.' This inspired us to create the simple secondary tool *Finding the pragmatic middle* to refer to in tough times.

Finding the pragmatic middle

This tool, in the form of a simple model, provides a handy reminder when you find yourself in an emotionally challenging situation.

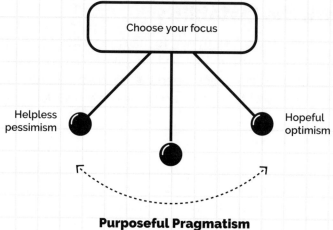

Purposeful Pragmatism

INSTRUCTIONS

1. When a situation occurs where you need to focus on the here and now and not get caught up in hopeful optimism or helpless pessimism, refer to this model.

2. Use it to remind yourself to deal with the realities in front of you now. Make the best of the situation and do what you need to do without letting your mind drift to speculation about the 'what if' of the future.

Purposeful pragmatism offers advantage over hope, as Paul Ostrowski regularly reminds himself and his team at Care Connect. 'Hope is not a strategy, and yet in really turbulent times it's one of those things that we tend to hold onto. That's fine but we can't define ourselves by hope; we must define ourselves by our intent and our actions.'

For leaders the Stockdale Paradox is a helpful reminder of the paradox that your role is to control in an environment where much is out of your control.

At the Australian Grand Prix Corporation, Andrew Westacott's approach aligns with purposeful pragmatism. 'We had to control the uncontrollable, which is a bit of a paradox, but what I mean is people can jump at shadows and get very defensive and protective. You need a mindset about accepting risk and taking constructive leadership right across your span of influence.'

Sometimes many things will be outside your control. When times are tough, confronting reality and focusing on what you can do (and control) now is the best way to optimise performance and wellbeing. As Voltaire said, 'Uncertainty is an uncomfortable position. But certainty is an absurd one.'

Core principles

You can strengthen your leadership toolkit to help you live with the paradox of controlling in an environment where much is out of your control and hopes can be dashed.

This is a life skill, not just something for the workplace. Every parent of a teenager needs this superpower, just as anyone facing illness or grief can benefit from the mindset and tools for navigating uncertainty and mastering the art of making peace with loss.

Two core principles and associated tools will help you to do exactly that in work and in life:

Principle 1	Principle 2
Embrace the highway of uncertainty	*Deal with loss*

Principle 1. Embrace the highway of uncertainty

For acclaimed design house IDEO, embracing ambiguity is a core value that they 'take very seriously … inviting designers to go with the flow in the face of the unknown', though they also acknowledge this as 'downright stress inducing'.

Psychologists support this view. We humans crave certainty. We don't like hovering in uncertainty, even to the extent that stress levels often fall after the diagnosis of serious illness just because the uncertainty has been relieved.

The quest for certainty is a survival instinct. You must expect protective behaviours when VUCA introduces uncertainty and ambiguity and sustains it, because our threat response is designed for the occasional danger, but not all-day everyday triggers.

All this suggests most of us aren't natural friends with uncertainty, particularly when it takes the form of an unclear future — threats to health, disruption to careers, economic volatility and so on.

We are wired to find our way back to certainty, and to see the black and white in the grey of paradoxes. We want certainty because it feels safer.

Crossing the highway of uncertainty

To strengthen your ability to let go and accept the externality of change we use a very effective metaphor based on real-life experience.

ADAPTABILITY

If you've ever visited Hanoi, Vietnam, you'll know that crossing the road can be a daunting task. With few traffic lights or pedestrian crossings, you must rely on your instincts and adaptability to make it across the street.

Chances are your first instinct is to watch the locals. They approach the kerb, check there are no large trucks coming and then launch confidently straight into the always-flowing multi-lane traffic, while motorbikes and cars peel off around them like a school of fish around a rock.

Now it's your turn. Assume the road you are crossing is called the *highway of uncertainty*! You'll be in Hanoi for a few days, so it is to your advantage to learn how to cross the road safely, given that the linear option of a controlled crossing to give you certainty and security isn't available.

You have three basic choices on crossing the highway of uncertainty:

>   » **Avoid.** Do everything possible to avoid crossing, or if essential, hide in a group so you can't see what's approaching on the road.

>   » **Join in.** Join in and learn to cross by doing it a few times to build confidence in reading the ebb and flow of the traffic and in your own approach.

>   » **Lead.** Do as the locals do by choosing to cross whenever you want, with whomever you want and at the pace that you choose with suitable awareness of the risks, such as big trucks.

CHOICES

These are precisely the same choices you have when facing uncertainty in the workplace. Just as the Hanoi locals have learned to let go of fear and to trust their own adaptability to navigate the uncertainty of the road, so can you when encountering those 'workplace highways'. The key is to be aware of your current relationship with uncertainty, to accept the squirm of joining in and learning, and finally to take the lead by welcoming the opportunities of uncertainty.

The primary tool *Cross the highway of uncertainty* will help you to:

>   » reflect on the approach you take to uncertainty

>   » identify strengths and areas of potential development

>   » build a more constructive relationship with uncertainty.

Cross the highway of uncertainty

The purpose of this tool is to boost awareness of your relationship with uncertainty and to gain confidence in navigating the pathway from disruption through adaptation to advantage. The instructions step you through the process and the model provides the framework.

INSTRUCTIONS

1. **View the highway of uncertainty.** The model describes three ways in which you might approach uncertainty. Take a few moments to familiarise yourself with each of the three approaches. Be mindful that your relationship with uncertainty isn't fixed and will change as circumstances change. For example, you might lead through uncertainty when working in your field of expertise, join in to explore something ambiguous in a cross-functional team setting, and avoid when uncertainty is imposed on you, such as leaders not providing a clear set of priorities.

2. **Reflect on your approach.** Following the model are three sets of reflection questions where you think of situations you have avoided, joined in and led through uncertainty.

3. **Calibrate your mindset.** After completing the reflection questions identify at least one strength you can rely on when uncertainty increases, and one area where you could become more open to joining in or taking the lead in uncertain or ambiguous conditions.

4. **Test and learn new habits.** The final step is to act by joining in or leading in a situation in the near future to build new habits.

Avoid if at all possible
Treat uncertainty as bad
Get certainty ASAP
Resist or dismiss ideas
Try to find a right way
Solve any paradoxes

Welcome the uncertainty
Be creative
Embrace the unknown
Experiment and learn
Be willing to not know
Innovate the paradoxes

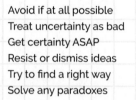

Choose to have a go
Watch and learn from others
Be open to possibilities
Adapt with the conditions
Try to enjoy the experience
Hold the tension on paradoxes

REFLECT

Experiences of uncertainty

Recall three different situations where you took an Avoid, Join In or Lead approach into uncertainty.

	Avoid	Join In	Lead
What were you thinking and feeling?			
What actions did you take or not take that impacted your effectiveness?			

» What is one strength you can rely on when uncertainty increases, and one area where you could become more open to joining in or taking the lead in uncertain conditions?

» What one action will you take to build an effective habit?

Remember the adaptive squirm

In situations of uncertainty and ambiguity the squirm is not knowing, because leaders are supposed to know!

The old leadership 'playbooks' said you are supposed to know the answer to the sales forecast, to how staff will react to pending cost cutting, and to the way forward on any and all of those adaptive challenges on your to-do list!

As an adaptive leader, your success lies in being open and vulnerable in acknowledging that you don't have all the answers, and in being more realistic with yourself about what you should know and control.

To lead with poise through uncertainty and ambiguity is to hold the tension or discomfort of not knowing, or of paradoxes that don't have right or wrong answers.

Here's a great reminder from Leukaemia Foundation CEO Chris Tanti: 'It's not going to be linear, so don't beat yourself up.'

Principle 2. Deal with loss

'Every act of creation is first an act of destruction.'
Pablo Picasso

Uncontrollable change is a feature of the constant flux of the modern workplace, but there is loss associated with change; as Picasso suggested, something gets destroyed.

Change the organisation structure, change leaders, merge, cut or grow and there is loss. Of course, that's not necessarily negative, because there are also new opportunities and relationships, and added value, but to take on uncontrollable change you must have the mental tools to deal with loss.

Letting go means loss

Accepting loss isn't a new idea. Swiss-American psychiatrist Elisabeth Kübler-Ross described five stages of grief in her ground-breaking 1969 book *On Death and Dying*. These were *denial, anger, bargaining, depression* and *acceptance*. While not a linear model, the Kübler-Ross Change Curve has been used effectively for decades to support people through many kinds of loss. Many organisations drew on this model or adaptations of it during the pandemic to explain and help staff explore and understand the feelings associated with the many real and feared losses. Some of those losses were physical, such as the death of loved ones and friends, while others were psychological, such as the loss of personal freedoms and routines, predictability, social contact, and future hopes and dreams.

The Kübler-Ross model is useful, as are many of the popular change management frameworks, in providing a mental model to understand and guide the journey through change. We believe William Bridges hit the nail on the head, though, with a simple game-shifting paradigm he called Transitions.

This paradigm distinguished between the physical events of change (such as job role) and the emotional or psychological journey of change (from the old to the new).

Bridges was perhaps the first to highlight the essential role that psychological loss and adjustment plays in organisational change when he observed, 'It isn't the changes that do you in, it's the transitions. Transition is the psychological process that people go through to come to terms with the new situation. Change is external, transition is internal.'

This notion of psychological loss is particularly relevant for advantage leaders because the pathway requires adjustment to the losses from disruption, adaptation from old ways to new ways, and a willingness to seek and gain advantage.

Martin has often reflected that some of the hardest aspects of the disruption in recent years have been the lost hopes, innovations and plans. Without the ability to make peace with loss and to transition through adaptation, there can be no advantage, but this is neither easy nor comfortable.

The pathway and loss

Disruption and adaptation are the first two phases of the pathway, and while they are anything but linear, they require letting go or leaving something behind.

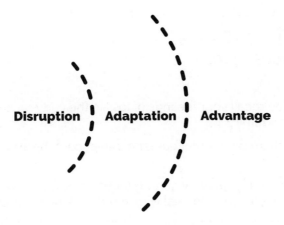

Disruption   Adaptation   Advantage

To grasp this process of letting go on the *highway of uncertainty* it can be helpful to step through the three phases and reflect on your approach to loss and moving on.

PHASE 1. DISRUPTION

Disruption can take away both the physical and the psychological. For example, the fears of generative AI are partly about the physical loss of jobs and personal security, but they are equally about the psychological threat response: fear of loss of control, autonomy, competence and so on.

To join in and lead disruption you must release and let go of loss. That can mean letting go of connections, relationships, roles, routines and habits, even your sense of identity.

You can hear that in Andrew Westacott's reflection on how he adapted and grew as a leader over the pandemic and beyond: 'I bring more patience now. We've still got a non-negotiable deadline and Formula 1® is about precision, but when I'm coaching my people I'm very aware to be open to different ways to achieve what we're ultimately all here to do.'

The loss from disruption can generate feelings of sadness, anger, denial or even relief, and you have to go through those to successfully adapt.

> **REFLECT**
> *Experiences of loss*
>
> » Can you recall your feelings of loss in the early days of the pandemic?
>
> » Have there been other career experiences where you faced loss?
>
> » Is there a disruption occurring for you now and if so, what loss will you need to deal with in order to move forward?

PHASE 2. ADAPTATION

Disruption is what pushes you onto the highway of uncertainty, and adaptation is your walk across it.

Stepping into the new can feel very uncomfortable, uncertain and something of an emotional roller coaster. It can be alluring to go back because there is anxiety and uncertainty about the future. However, adaptation doesn't happen if you avoid the reality. You must embrace whatever is new, which might mean a new role, different relationships or perhaps a new identity.

Adaptation has its own pace, requiring both personal reflection and shared conversations. Among the massive changes being driven across the defence sector and her organisation, Tanya Monro observes, 'I have found it important at times to go slow to go faster; to take the time we need to prioritise the overt conversations needed to align assumptions across our leaders and teams.'

REFLECT
Your adaptations

» Recall some of your adaptations to different roles, relationships and circumstances in recent years. What do they tell you about how you joined in or led?

» Have you experienced an adaptation of identity, such as through marriage, having a child or changing career course? What happened to your mindset?

When you adapt it is because you embrace a different future and let go of the past, or at least put it into a place where it allows you to move on.

PHASE 3. ADVANTAGE

Advantage happens when you have let go of the losses of disruption, joined in on the 'highway' and have been driven forward by hope, energy and creativity. New habits and practices emerge and you learn and grow. This is adaptive mindset in action, as illustrated by the *Working model adaptive mindset* introduced in chapter 4.

Advantage comes from unlocking potential in your organisation and its people and embracing change. As City of Melbourne Lord Mayor Sally Capp explains about the impacts and outcomes of the pandemic, 'It's completely changed the paradigm, and it's not settled. We had to become a City of Yes, and we are trying to capture more of that as we go forward.'

> ## REFLECT
> *Embracing the future*
>
> »   Where have you turned disruption into advantage?
>
> »   What mindset works best for you to move beyond adaptation and to take the lead in shaping new paradigms or finding new opportunities? What loss have you accepted in doing so?
>
> »   Is there an insight or lesson from these reflections that will help you to lead others through adversity?

Control is overrated. Cross the highway

Earlier in this chapter we posed the question: How do you maintain a healthy sense of control, confidence and agency that is suited to the shifting norms of a post-pandemic world?

Anna Wenngren: 'From a leadership perspective it's very much about awareness that we can't solve the external problems outside of our control, but we can certainly talk to our people about what we are doing to navigate that, and what is in our control.'

You can be sure that change is a constant and that it will often be beyond your control, which makes it essential to embrace uncertainty and take the lead rather than avoid it.

Now you face a paradox because while you cannot control everything, you do have agency and there are things you can control. Accept this paradox and be open to navigating loss at a pace that works for you and those you lead. You can and will turn disruption to advantage.

Learnings

» An **optimistic** frame of mind means seeing solutions instead of problems and treating setbacks as temporary. If **pessimism** prevails, however, you will see all-pervasive problems and defeat in every direction.

» Your leadership role is to **control** in an environment where much is out of your control. **Purposeful pragmatism** works well.

» On the **highway of uncertainty** you have choices:

  » **Avoid.** Do everything possible to avoid crossing.

  » **Join in.** Learn by experimenting to build confidence in reading and adapting to the ebb and flow.

  » **Lead.** Choose to go wherever and whenever you want, with whomever you want, and at your own pace, all with a suitable awareness of risks posed.

» To lead with poise through uncertainty and ambiguity is to **hold the tension** or discomfort of not knowing, or of paradoxes that don't have right or wrong answers.

» Without the ability to **accept loss** there can be no advantage. This is neither easy nor comfortable, however. It requires courage, experience, persistence and learning.

CHAPTER 8

Dial up the learning

What is your single most important capability when facing adaptive challenges? How do you learn and adapt at pace when there is so much information to absorb? How do you know what is going on when change can happen anywhere at any time?

Loops and insights

From the late 1700s until the early 1990s, the multi-volume *Encyclopedia Britannica* was the trusted source for learning for millions of people around the world. The vastness and linear nature of its content was reflected in the achievement of American author and businessman Amos Shirk, who claims to have read the entire 23-volume 1911 edition from cover to cover in four and a half years, devoting roughly three hours per night to the project.

Three waves of technology accelerated the collapse of the traditional *Encyclopedia Britannica* market. First came personal computers shipped with CD-ROMs complete with sound, video and animations, which transformed learning in households traditionally visited by the famous door-to-door encyclopedia sales force. Then, internet search engines and, more specifically, Wikipedia democratised knowledge acquisition and ended the dominance of *Britannica* and the CD-ROM.

Today, the third wave of large language learning systems such as ChatGPT is sweeping across and disrupting industries such as education, finance, healthcare and media.

When Captain Sullivan had seconds to weigh up the situation on board QF72, he could hardly reach for an encyclopedia. He was trying to make sense of what the military call an 'asymmetric situation', where plans, resources and controls no longer match what is happening. He had just moments to sort through a lifetime of gathered information, knowledge and experience, decide what he believed to be most applicable, then respond, before adapting again as the context continued to change.

While you are unlikely to be piloting a passenger jet in danger of dropping out of the sky, you are in an unpredictable and fast-changing world where encyclopedias certainly aren't the answer, but neither is being overwhelmed by the constantly expanding universe of information and resources at your digital fingertips.

You can turn these situations to advantage by calibrating your mindset to two foundational ideas: *Apply the discipline of loops* to accelerate and sustain the pace at which you can learn and adapt, and *Get insights from the field* to understand what's really going on, instead of what the structures, systems and processes indicate.

To help set the scene, before moving to those two important topics, a little background on pace and learning would be useful.

The pace is on

We recently asked a forum of more than 50 leaders whether they felt the pace of work had increased, decreased or stayed roughly the same in the past five years. More than 90 per cent said they thought it had increased.

When quizzed about what had changed, the answers fell into two categories, the first group of responses were as we expected: pressure to be competitive, rapid changes in technology, shorter cycle times for new products and so on. The second group were more intriguing and can be summed up by a question posed by one participant: 'Is it just me,' they asked, 'or is time going faster?'

Perception of pace is one thing, but what has really accelerated the game is the less linear environment with its inherent nonlinear challenges and driving forces.

hummgroup Group CEO Rebecca James points to one of the greatest driving forces as the impact of social media: 'Even in capital markets the speed of collapses is happening at a pace which has just never been seen before.'

Anna Wenngren notes what the capital crunch in tech means for SafetyCulture: 'The biggest mindset shift is how we get speed. Previously to get something done, we would invest in headcount. Now we don't have that luxury; it's about how to do more with less.'

Adapting to these shifts requires constant, dynamic learning. Simply put, if you can't learn at pace then you can't adapt at pace, let alone gain advantage from disruption.

This is a big mindset shift because learning in the workplace has long been associated with training courses, data sets, post-project reviews, and performance and development systems. In other words, in a linear environment you can plan for learning because goals and desired outcomes are clear, things happen in sequence with a good level of predictability, and the connection between cause and effect helps and guides people to learn.

Nonlinear environments upend expectations about learning because unexpected experiences and outcomes emerge in complex and unpredictable ways, which means learning has to be dynamic to suit the context.

Different mindset and tools are needed. Here are two that are essential for advantage leaders:

Apply the discipline of loops	Get insights from the field
Accelerate and sustain the pace at which you learn and adapt.	Understand what's really going on instead of what the system wants you to know.

Apply the discipline of loops

For a core framework we go to the cutting edge of world sport, where technology meets world-class performance, then back to the 1980s and a well-known concept and tool that provides exactly the principles needed to build the right mindset.

When Emirates New Zealand won the 2021 America's Cup, attention turned to their partnership with McKinsey and to the AI bot developed to fast-track learning about how to adapt the boat to suit the conditions. By simulating racing at ten times the speed of a human sailor, Emirates New Zealand simply learned faster than their competitors.

Learning happens in a loop and McKinsey gave the sailors a faster and better learning loop.

What's in that loop?

The answer to that question can be found in manufacturing in the 1980s, when industry embraced learning loops to improve the quality of processes through continual learning and adapting. The authorship and evolution of the tool is shared between two founders of the quality movement, Walter Shewhart and Edwards Deming. The tool is known by the acronym PDCA, which stands for *Plan, Do, Check, Adapt*, and is essentially the scientific method (see figure 8.1).

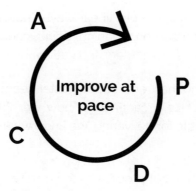

Figure 8.1: The PDCA loop

With an overarching goal to win the America's Cup and the intent to make the boat go faster, the sailing team basically spun the PDCA learning loop multiple times by:

» *planning* — deciding on adaptations to boat and sail

» *doing* — running the simulation

» *checking* — evaluating and learning about impacts

» *adapting* — making changes, and repeating the PDCA over and over again.

The business world is also adopting faster loops, and the change is stark.

Like most senior leaders, Martin circa 2019 began his year with a meeting with each direct report to agree on annual objectives and discuss a career plan. Every month he checked in against progress and a mid-year review formally recorded progress against plan. The year closed with the annual performance review, when career plans were reviewed and updated.

COVID dramatically changed the tempo; monthly check-ins, in some cases, became daily. All advantage leaders report similar experiences.

There's no going back to the old 'linear' ways. The new way means fast, disciplined loops focused on planning, doing, checking and adapting, applied to self, team, stakeholders and deliverables.

Paul Ostrowski, who has embedded faster learning loops in Care Connect, observes, 'It's a cadence of how we hold each other and ourselves accountable for delivering. We know when we're off track and can adapt fast.'

And it's not so much about process as the quality of the conversations that close the loop and reset for the next cycle.

Andrew McConville operates a weekly cadence one-to-one with each direct report. 'It's half an hour, no agenda, just opening with "How's it going?" and then lots of open-ended questions about what's been good, what's difficult and what do we need to do different. And I always close with "Anything I can do to help?", because it's important they feel supported as leaders.'

There's a mix of informality and one critical ingredient, *discipline*, because the key to success in high-demand environments is the quality of those learning loops.

Advantage leaders are looking not just to learn at speed but to grow their people at speed because it's a business imperative. Brett Wickham, at ACCIONA Energia Australia: 'I should be growing people around me anywhere in the business. Trying to get them to grow to a point where they're going to take the next challenge.'

Loop and learn shortcuts

In chapter 13 you will learn about tools and approaches to accelerating team learning; in this section, however, our focus is on recalibrating mindset, and for that we bring together a variety of items recommended by advantage leaders with loop and learn practices and shortcuts, for your reflection and action.

This is a set of activities to stimulate your thinking about calibrating mindset towards using loops to learn at pace. Work through each of the sub-items identified in figure 8.2, including the secondary tool *Basics of PDCA*. Look for opportunities to bring any insights or learning into your daily habits and routines, so you can sustain these in high-demand situations.

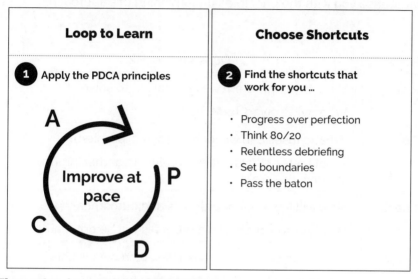

Figure 8.2: loop to learn shortcuts

Shortcut 1. Apply the PDCA principles

The PDCA cycle is all about continuous learning and adaptation. Basically, you go through loops where you try something, see how it works, then make improvements based on what you've learned. It's a way to keep getting better over time. The PDCA principles are:

» **P**lan: Establish your aim and plan.

» **D**o: Implement and take action.

» **C**heck: Measure and evaluate results.

» **A**dapt: Adjust plan based on results.

For continuous improvement, repeat by iterating to improve over time.

Basics of PDCA

This secondary tool is intended to guide you through an activity to familiarise you with the principles underpinning this approach.

PDCA	Questions to ask
Plan	What is the problem we are looking to solve?
	What will 'solved' look like?
Do	What causes can we identify for this problem?
	What tests or trials will we conduct to gather information to solve the problem?
Check	How will we monitor progress and outcomes?
	What tempo of checking progress will be optimal?
Adapt	What changes will we make based on our insights?
	Is there another PDCA loop to test further?

INSTRUCTIONS

1. Use this tool with your team to introduce the idea of learning loops.

2. Choose a work-based problem or issue, and explain you intend to facilitate a PDCA loop to tackle the issue.

3. Introduce your team to the basic principles of PDCA.

4. Work through the loop using the questions above as the basic framework.

5. After completing a full loop debrief the experience, including discussing opportunities to build loops into ways of operating.

Shortcut 2. Choose shortcuts

Here are five shortcuts that are commonly used by advantage leaders to accelerate their learning and adaptability.

PROGRESS OVER PERFECTION

State Library Victoria CEO Paul Duldig mentioned the phrase 'progress over perfection' when sharing his experiences leading through turbulence. For him it means being okay with how things are done provided they are effective. He acknowledges this has been a big shift in mindset. *Are you holding onto standards that no longer suit the world in which you are now working?*

THINK 80/20

Arguably the most popular shortcut is the Pareto principle, named after Italian economist Vilfredo Pareto, who observed that 80 per cent of the land in Italy was owned by 20 per cent of the population. The business equivalent is that 20 per cent of efforts yields 80 per cent of the results. The trick is to find the 20 per cent, and reduce the less effective 80 per cent, and it takes judgement and some appetite for risk to do that. *How's your 80/20 thinking?*

RELENTLESS DEBRIEFING

The 'action debrief' is a trademark practice of elite units in the military, emergency medicine and sporting teams. This is the pause to capture insights and adjust based on what's been learned and what's happening. 'When things are tough harness the learned experiences of the organisation,' advises advantage leader Robert Iervasi. *Do you take time to reflect, learn and adapt?* We cover this in detail in chapter 13.

SET BOUNDARIES

What are the important boundaries for a leader? For example, setting limits on availability, making time for deep work, and outlining decision-making authority and delegations. *What are your boundaries? How do you know when enough is enough? Do your boundaries help or hinder your adaptability?* In the next chapter we challenge you to prioritise self-care, and an important part of that is setting boundaries. Without boundaries you risk a lack of focus, burnout and other negative consequences.

PASS THE BATON

Pace doesn't just mean that you have to run faster. Business is like a relay, and it can be helpful to remember that it's not how fast you run in a relay, but rather how fast the baton moves. *Are you too often the lone runner instead of being part of a relay team? Where are the opportunities to partner with others to accelerate the planning, doing, checking and adapting?*

REFLECT
Your shortcuts

Take a few moments to reflect on your mindset and habits in each of the shortcuts we have just covered. Rate from 1 = *No change needed* to 5 = *Big change needed.*

Boundaries	1	2	3	4	5
Progress over perfection	O	O	O	O	O
Thinking 80/20	O	O	O	O	O
Relentlessly debriefing	O	O	O	O	O
Setting boundaries	O	O	O	O	O
Passing the baton	O	O	O	O	O

Get insights from the field

An adaptive mindset includes using game-changing insights in real time from staff, colleagues, customers, stakeholders and competitors to supplement your usual business systems and processes.

Sally Capp: 'It's the frequency, the immediacy, the openness to get the right sort of feedback from as many people as possible.'

Combined together, *hard data plus insights* will help you to learn and adapt at accelerated pace.

The usual range of metrics covering people, customers, processes and the broader environment set the baseline for decision making, but two crucial ingredients are easily missed:

» the *unspoken* — the unstated yet important ideas and feelings of people that don't get raised with you because for one reason or another people choose not to speak up

» the *unnoticed* — signals and patterns that get lost in the noise of everything else that is happening around you and your team.

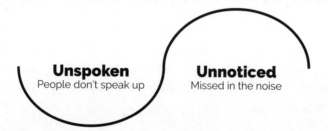

Unspoken
People don't speak up

Unnoticed
Missed in the noise

Without tools to bring these two elements to the surface you risk missing important information about everything from safety to breakthrough innovations.

What are you missing?

With the rate of change accelerating, how can you be sure that:

» your last employee satisfaction survey is actually telling you how your workforce is feeling today

» you know what customers are thinking about their next purchase

» you know whether strategic partners are still on the same page?

No doubt you have limited time to pore over mountains of data about engagement and alignment, which is fine because the secret to effectiveness isn't just the flow of feedback, it's the combination of solid data and human insights.

Insights are the equivalent of reading the room — a doctor sensing a small change in a patient's manner, a skilled police officer watching for shifts in the mood of a crowd and adapting accordingly, or a conductor tuning into texture and tone and making fine adjustments to lift the orchestra.

This is not only about reading insights; it's also about shaping the environment to make it more likely that insights will emerge.

The doctor uses care and empathy to build trust with the patient so they feel safer to share feelings; the police officer learns the cultural norms of the community and becomes a part of it; the conductor creates a language of subtle movements understood in the moment by the orchestra.

What has this got to do with pragmatic day-to-day business?

Everything. One poignant example is situated at the intersection of aircraft failure and culture change.

Amy Edmondson introduced the concept of *psychological safety* — the shared belief that you won't be penalised or shamed for speaking up with ideas, questions, concerns or mistakes. She described in a *Harvard Business Review* article how aircraft manufacturer Boeing became aware that a potential cause of two fatal accidents on 737 MAX jets was an 'overly ambitious production schedule and [people] fearful of losing their jobs if they raised concerns'.

Fast forward three years and Boeing had successfully embedded a cultural norm to speak up and in doing so transformed the way the company operates.

Insights tell you what's really going on

Insights are what you need to solve nonlinear problems, to unlock potential and to take things to a new level.

Insights help you to know what's really going on, rather than what is supposed to be going on or what people want you to think is going on.

Robert Iervasi offers an important perspective: 'Never rely on a single version of truth. Make sure you are getting information from lots of sources to triage, almost like an emergency department, what the right course of action would be.'

Researchers Philip Boxer and Carole Eigen used the acronym 'WIGO' (What Is Going On) to highlight how leaders get filtered information. The takeaway? Leaders must be deliberate in drawing out unfiltered insights from the field or they won't know WIGO.

Training the habit of insights

To be a master of insights is not to accept everything you find — quite the opposite.

Paul Duldig issues a warning: 'In turbulence you hear a lot of interpretations when data emerges. It can be from anywhere and the first comment you hear is, "That's because . . .". 'It's feeding confirmation bias and trying to make things look linear and predictable when that's not what's really happening. You need to stay open to alternative perspectives, to that sense of 'what's going on', not what someone thinks or wants you to think is going on.'

WIGO indeed. Let's build some habits.

Start with curiosity

Curiosity is the gateway to the world of insights, but it's a gate we risk closing when attuned to solving linear problems with an expert mindset.

Here are two perspectives of leaders showing curiosity:

Those in favour...	Those against...
Curiosity shows you are interested and open to alternatives. It suggests humility and transparency, while increasing your understanding of different world views. It makes you wiser, and the good news is that curious people are actually happier, often because others know they care.	Curiosity shows you don't know the answer. It opens you to criticism for procrastinating or being uncertain or, worse still, incompetent. Is that all? Not quite, because apparently curiosity killed the cat. Which means keep out of other people's business, don't ask questions that don't concern you and stay in your own lane.

Unfortunately, there is a lot of cultural inertia in the case against. Don't give the boss bad news, keep your head down, let them sort it out, it's not our problem, there are no prizes for raising problems unless they're obvious, it's above my pay grade and so on.

Cynical? Yes, but with even a hint of these thoughts, the mindset you (or your team) bring will be protective rather than curious.

Our aim is to strengthen your awareness of the benefits of gaining insight and help you to generate insights from as far and wide as possible. To do that you need a mindset and the accompanying habits to seek, absorb and act on insights.

Habit 1	Habit 2	Habit 3
SEEK	*ABSORB*	*ACT*
Find WIGO	Generate insights	Take calculated risks

Habit 1. Seek insights

To find out what's going on you must create relationships in which people don't fear you or feel the need to protect themselves or you by putting up a facade or holding back.

Paul Duldig describes it as being 'emotionally available', meaning you show your humanity and vulnerability. Paul Ostrowski notes that one of the benefits of the COVID experience was deeper personal relationships with his team, which fostered more open conversations. We explore this concept of vulnerability in depth in chapter 14.

Develop the habit of being open and curious in your interactions with others and deliberate in going to the 'edges' of your organisation. Try these:

» Interact more directly with customers.

» Listen to the experiences of staff at all levels and in all areas.

» Engage with the hopes and concerns of stakeholders.

Advantage leaders seek insight opportunities, like regular coffee catch-ups with a random selection of staff and engaging more closely with stakeholders. Kate Koch from SEEK: 'Stakeholder relationships are vital and it's essential to invest time in those relationships and not wait until a transaction is needed.'

In a nonlinear world the demands or threats can come from anywhere. By getting closer to the edges of your organisation, you not only improve your understanding, but also make it more likely that the scouts will make you aware when stuff happens that isn't supposed to happen.

REFLECT
Your habits

The following practices are important for gaining insight from the field. Assess your current performance in using these habits using the rating scale 1 = Never to 5 = Always.

Ask yourself, what could I change right now that would allow me to be more effective in gaining insight into my organisation and beyond?

Habits to seek insights	1	2	3	4	5
Listen without judgement. Stay open to exploring ideas and options rather than making assumptions.	o	o	o	o	o
Show you are open to being wrong. Don't feel you need to be right all the time. Say 'I don't know' when you don't.	o	o	o	o	o
Open things up. Read the room and pause a meeting to check in when the tone suggests there is something unspoken.	o	o	o	o	o
Go to the edge. Spend time with staff, and engage with partners one-to-one about their hopes and concerns.	o	o	o	o	o
Be in the moment. Resist the temptation to multi-task. Give people your undivided attention.	o	o	o	o	o

Habit 2. Absorb insights

When you generate insights from the field, it is important to give yourself the best chance of absorbing what you hear and see so you can turn them into insights.

Neuroscience researchers identify three states associated with insights: having a quiet mind, inner reflection and seeding the need without striving too hard for a solution. The latter means taking in questions about problems and opportunities and then trusting your mind to find an insight. Creatives might describe this as being patient and open to the muse, others might recognise it as the moment of inspiration in the shower.

It's worth considering how you might find more time for these three practices:

Quiet mind	How can you better align quiet time with issues that require insights?
Personal reflection	What subtle shift in your daily schedule would create time for inner reflection rather than focusing on external events?
Open, not pushing	How can you 'seed the need' and patiently stay open for insights?

REFLECT
Daily practices

Think about your daily schedule and its routines and rituals.

» Do you give yourself a chance to practise these three states?

» Could busyness and efficiency be blocking you from your best 'aha' moments?

» What insights does this generate?

Habit 3. Act on insights

To give yourself the best chance of turning insights into action you'll need to consider your own risk appetite or, in other words, your tolerance for potential losses. Sally Capp: 'Do things and create momentum. Because, frankly, it helps you move on quickly to better decisions and better outcomes, but sometimes that's the pain on the way through.'

Acting on insights can certainly trigger that defensive mindset, so here's a chance to pause and reflect on your risk appetite.

REFLECT
Risk appetite

Reflect on any insights you have gathered but haven't yet acted upon in your work. Focus on the ones where you have a sense there could be a mix of value and risk.

Use figure 8.3 as your reference then consider the questions below.

» What is your tolerance for risk in those situations?

» Is your tolerance at the level you want, or would you like to change it in some way?

» What new habit might help shift your level of tolerance? (For example, you might decide to delegate more to your team and accept more risk.)

Tolerance for risk			
Very low	**Low**	**Moderate**	**High**
Risk averse; dislike uncertainty; avoid risk in decisions	Cautious; prefer ultrasafe options; keep risk as low as possible in decisions	Willing to accept risk; weigh up decisions to find right balance of risk and return	Innovative in dealing with risk; look for higher returns by accepting risk

Figure 8.3: tolerance for risk

Recap

Advantage leaders gather insights from the field by listening to employees, customers and other stakeholders. This helps them to know what is going on so they can adapt to the rapidly changing environment and base decisions on current and relevant information.

Insights from the field also build trust, engagement and accountability among employees, and help to foster a more open culture of innovation and continuous improvement. By leveraging these insights, you are better placed to navigate challenges in a resilient and responsive way.

Learnings

» In nonlinear environments learning must be **dynamic** to suit the unpredictable and complex nature of the conditions.

» **Learning at pace** is the single most important skill to enable adaptability in a turbulent environment.

» You have limited time to pore over mountains of information so it's important to get savvy at **seeking**, **absorbing** and **acting** on insights to get ahead of the game.

» Invest in **learning loops** like PDCA for yourself, your team and your stakeholders so you align, collaborate and learn at pace.

» An adaptive mindset requires using **game-changing insights** in real time from staff, colleagues, customers, stakeholders and competitors to supplement your usual business systems and processes.

» Insights help you to know **what is going on** and not what others or the system want you to know.

» Insights from the field also aid in fostering a more **open culture** of innovation and continuous improvement.

CHAPTER 9

Prioritise self-care

How do you sustain performance and wellbeing in a high-demand environment? What are the costs of ignoring self-care? Is it important or just a luxury? Are there self-care practices that suit the demands of high-performing advantage leaders? What benefits can self-care have beyond oneself?

In the iconic *7 Habits of Highly Effective People*, Stephen Covey chose for the final habit 'Sharpen the Saw' and urged us to celebrate it as the habit that made all the others possible.

To sharpen the saw you must invest in what we now call *self-care*. It's about refreshing and renewing personal energy in all its forms. Covey acknowledged how hard it can be to prioritise this investment in the face of the urgent demands of everyday life.

Performance *and* wellbeing

Professional tennis players travel the world month on month competing in ATP events spread across more than 30 countries. Performance is the currency of success. Take a Grand Slam like Wimbledon, for example. The draw starts with 128 players. How many matches does it take to decide a winner? The answer is simple: 127. Why simple? Because 127 players will lose their last match in the tournament, leaving one unbeaten winner.

Tennis is tough. You win and you advance. You lose and it's back on a plane and off to the next hotel, the next practice court, the next doping control and so on.

Even the best players find it tough. Roger Federer, speaking at a Uniqlo press conference in Tokyo, highlighted the intense pressure on players: 'As a tennis player, you're always thinking about your next practice, your next match. It never lets you go.'

Tennis is not alone in its gruelling schedule. Just about every top sport now loads up its program to meet the insatiable demands of media, fans and the sponsors that feed off them.

Fatigue, injuries, burnout and sport science research have all played a part in transforming the elite sport training environment. Old ways of loading up physical training to achieve peak performance have been remodelled in a new paradigm in which balance between performance and wellbeing is key, and mindset tools and techniques are prized:

Performance + Wellbeing = Thrive in turbulence

Ongoing workplace turbulence compels advantage leaders to consider using those high-performance insights and tools to sustain performance and wellbeing through everything from the disruptions of pandemics, cyber-attacks and media pile-ons to the ongoing pressures of new technologies, workforce shortages and the relentless pace of change.

High performance is a necessity, but it can't be sustained on the inevitable roller coaster of ups and downs without prioritising physical and mental wellbeing. Here's how to calibrate your mindset towards performance and wellbeing by prioritising self-care.

Know your energy patterns and habits

Leadership requires a lot of physical, mental and emotional energy. There's the personal workload, the nurturing and motivating of a team, engaging with a network of colleagues, stakeholders and customers, and the continual requirement to learn and adapt. And that's just the work part, without any of the essential commitments to family, friends and community.

Where does your energy come from and what do you do on a regular basis to maintain and enhance your overall health and wellbeing?

When asked of leaders and business professionals this question often draws a blank or a somewhat guilty look, perhaps because the first casualty of increased turbulence is often self-care. The pattern goes something like this:

»   Workload increases, which takes more time (energy out).

»   Healthy habits like exercising and relaxing are sidelined to fit in other demands (less energy in).

»   Reserves of energy drop and stress and fatigue set in, often accompanied by less healthy habits that mask the symptoms (energy depleted).

A new pattern is soon established, and it's double trouble because not only has the load increased but the habits that previously helped body and mind to rest, reset and rejuvenate are gone.

For a high-performing leader this raises two important questions that, as Covey suggested, are fundamental to sustaining everything else in a high-demand environment:

»   How do I minimise the risk of fatigue and, in a worst-case scenario, burnout?

»   How do I set myself up to sustain optimal energy?

Let's consider the question of burnout before applying a core sport psychology tool to understand and sustain high performance.

Beware the burnout threshold

Before the pandemic it was rare to hear a conversation about fatigue, other than at the back end of the year when deadlines loomed and holidays beckoned. Fatigue after a long year was expected, understood and to be assuaged by rest and recovery over the holidays.

COVID changed the language and meaning of fatigue, which is unquestionably one of the greatest by-products of the pandemic, as daily habits were upended, access to exercise reduced, anxiety about family and community heightened, and uncertainty rolled on. Of course, one of the most common symptoms of COVID itself is fatigue, and for those unfortunate enough to experience long COVID that's an ongoing battle.

Fatigue was to be expected but it has continued unabated as health professionals across the US, UK and Australia report exhaustion to be on the rise.

Stephen Covey might have called it a consequence of years of neglecting to 'sharpen the saw' caused by a mix of sub-par lifestyle habits and increased demands.

The consequences of burnout go well beyond workplace performance. Fatigue also creates health risks, ranging from the potential for depression to the physical effects of poor lifestyle habits.

The model in figure 9.1 is a handy way to reflect on your personal relationship to burnout and, more specifically, whether you are at risk of reaching the *burnout threshold*.

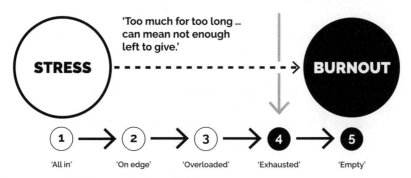

Figure 9.1: the burnout threshold

Warning signs on the pathway

Here's a typical business professional's journey along the burnout pathway. We will call him 'Alan'.

Alan wins an exciting new job and takes the first step (1) on the pathway. Alan is 'all in', embracing the job with boundless energy and complete commitment. He uses any down time to read up on new developments in the industry and to get ahead of the workload. Things are moving fast and well.

After a few months, Alan has dropped off previous habits around exercise and meditation, and the initial burst of freshness and excitement has mostly gone out of the job. A sense (2) of big possibilities is accompanied by feeling a bit pressured and on edge about the more complex aspects of the role.

Those issues settle but other challenges arise and the load continues to increase. Alan's time is consumed in meetings, coaching the team, and resolving tensions that break out all too regularly across the organisational silos. There doesn't seem to be time to get personal work done, let alone do something relaxing, although there is a holiday booked a few months away.

Alan has entered a day-to-day norm (3) of feeling overloaded by constant, relentless demands. Evenings and weekends are overrun by real work and overthinking. Maybe the holidays aren't really a good idea because the crises are coming thick and fast and need constant attention.

The warning signs are there for Alan, and they need attention because if this pattern continues there is a high risk of entering the threshold zone.

Alan takes just a portion of his planned holiday but stays connected the whole time and returns more irritated and out of balance than before. Soon the prolonged stress (4) catches up and the days get harder and harder as mental, physical and emotional reserves are depleted. He needs rest from this relentless pattern, but there's no escape, and the extra alcohol at night isn't helping. It feels like a vicious circle: get home, eat and drink, finish emails and work some more, drink more, argue with partner, sleep badly, wake tired, go to work.

During the day Alan tries to put on a confident facade, but it's wearing thin, as is shown in barely concealed frustration that affects conversations and damages relationships, leading to even more isolation.

Alan is on the verge of burnout (5), which will mean chronic tiredness and indifference. Severe depression is a real risk, and intervention is essential.

Fortunately, the awareness of and concern for the damaging effects of fatigue is much greater in organisations now than just a few years ago. The organisation intervenes and gets Alan professional help, which over time enables him to draw back from a dangerous edge and to develop a much more constructive and healthy approach to work.

Alan found help. The harsh reality, however, is that in many workplaces (and mindsets) leaders are expected to tough it out. 'They're paid more, so they should be able to handle it.'

Yes, leaders can expect a more demanding environment and that's fine if you have the tools, but not if, like Alan, your boundary is exhaustion, because once that line is crossed it's damned hard to go back.

REFLECT
Burnout threshold

Consider your boundaries and your current position on the *burnout threshold*.

- » What insights does the burnout threshold create for you?
- » What changes in habits will help you to find a healthy balance between energy in and energy out?
- » What support will help you put these ideas into action?

Attend to your inner game

Now-retired Formula 1® champion Sebastian Vettel could often be found just before qualifying sitting in a stationary car, eyes closed, visualising the lap ahead.

'Once you start the lap,' explains Vettel, 'there's no time to think so you clear your mind and you have to be in the moment. Even if you make a mistake, it's important not to think about it. You just focus corner by corner, ideally, let it flow.'

Vettel was seeking his 'zone'. Chances are you've heard tennis players, footballers or golfers reflecting on their performance and saying they were *'in the zone'*, that holy grail mindset of total immersion in the game with energy, rhythm and confidence flowing in the right way.

Have you had that 'zone' experience at work? Cutting through to the core of the most wicked of issues; soothing and repairing conflicts with calmness and composure; and presenting with such confidence and energy that you inspire your audience to take on the most challenging of concerns and land them with total agreement?

Peak zone and performance zone

If only every day was an *in-the-zone* day.

Maybe that's a little too optimistic; however, we are confident that if you apply some of the insights and training of high-performing athletes you will get better at finding the optimal zone.

There is one caution we would like to point out before you dive in. Unless you're an Olympic athlete or similar, it can be unhelpful to equate the zone with peak performance. For a start, you need to show up more often than once every four years! Peak experiences are notoriously hard to replicate, but if you dial it back a little there's lots you can learn from your own experiences at what we call 'A-game level'.

That's not the once-in-a–blue moon moment tennis champion Billie Jean King once described as so powerful. She said she wanted to stop the match to grab the microphone and shout, 'That's what it's all about!'

A-game level is what happens when you really do show up. Consider it your best 20 to 25 per cent performance. It's when you are clear-minded, fully engaged in the task and open to opportunity. It's when you bring your natural adaptive mindset — *constructive – courageous – creative*.

US lawyer Basil S Walsh might have had the A-game in mind when he said, 'We don't need more strength or more ability or greater opportunity. What we need is to use what we have.'

Indeed. Sometimes we go looking for tools and tactics we don't need. Your A-game is a great place to explore and unpack your best, to discover the triggers or blocks to showing up at your best.

They will help you understand your natural mindset and set you up to choose and apply self-care principles and practices in ways that suit you best.

A blueprint for your A-game

Take a moment to visualise this situation.

An important strategic planning meeting is about to begin. You are seated with a dozen or so colleagues around a large rectangular table readying for what will inevitably be difficult conversations and decisions about priorities, roles and structures. You pause for a moment to scan the team members.

Some are chatting with colleagues, a couple are hurriedly finishing off emails, and others are flicking through slides on screens in readiness for presentations and discussions to follow.

Imagine each of your colleagues has a bracelet on their wrist that registers one of three colours depending on the frame of mind they are in at that moment:

» **Blue bracelets** are thinking about achieving outcomes and building a stronger team and organisation. They're alert, energetic and confident. They feel at the top of their game and are looking forward to taking on the challenges of the day. They're open to tackling the biggest issues, very tuned into the team dynamics and keen to unlock potential.

» **Red bracelets** are thinking about winning or losing. They're more amped than the blue bracelets and feel edgy, impatient, even a bit frustrated. Their tone of voice sounds a bit intolerant, and they're more intent on making their point than listening or exploring what others think. They want outcomes provided they have control and certainty.

» **Green bracelets** are thinking they'd rather be somewhere else. They haven't brought the right energy, but rather fatigue, or more likely preoccupation with doubts and worries. They are cautious and tentative, keen to fit in and most likely will wait on others before committing to anything.

Mind zones

The bracelets describe three typical *mind zones*. Blue bracelet or blue zone is most characteristic of 'A-game level', while red and green doesn't automatically mean they won't do well, but they have a lower chance of success over time. Importantly, when in the blue zone people often report using less energy, or even gaining energy.

Do you notice feeling more in control of your game when you're in the blue zone?

Irrespective of whether your day requires facilitating a team meeting, having a high-stakes conversation or leaning into a really complex problem, it will seem easier in the blue zone.

Contrast that to times when you don't feel in control of your game and are a bit more 'red' or 'green'. Relationships seem strained and transactional, it's hard to connect the dots on complex issues, and it's easy to feel isolated and under siege.

That's why athletes train for the zone. They know they'll feel more in control of their game, with a clear and composed mind, focusing on what matters, making good choices and teaming with others, rather than a cluttered or hurried mind with its distractions, pressures and sense of conflict. This is the foundational sport psychology concept brought to attention by Mihaly Csikszentmihalyi in his book *Flow*.

REFLECT
Zone experiences

Take a few moments to consider these questions about your 'zone experiences':

» What coloured 'mind zone' have you brought to recent important meetings and conversations?

» Did it change colour during the meeting or in different situations?

» What colour is your zone when you are at A-game level?

» What are the pluses and minuses of being in the red and green zone?

Understanding your 'zones' and knowing what blocks and triggers them is key to self-care, so let's get into the primary tool *Self-care plan*.

Self-care plan

The purpose of this tool and the accompanying Self-care Canvas (overleaf) is to help you discover and understand the triggers to the three mind zones so you can plan and commit to optimal self-care habits.

INSTRUCTIONS

1. Print or draw the canvas and follow the three steps described.

2. The following pages explore the three steps with prompting questions and examples to guide your training:

    Step 1. Understand your blue, red and green zones.

    Step 2. Identify your A-game triggers and blockers.

    Step 3. Commit to self-care habits that trigger your zone.

    These three steps are commonly part of the mental training of professional sportspeople and are proven to help build effective habits to support performance and wellbeing.

Self-Care Canvas

Step 1
Understand

How you think, act and feel in this zone.

Step 2
Identify

Record what triggers this zone for you

Step 3
Commit

Commit to start, stop or continue to sustain self-care habits

Blue Zone

Red Zone

Green Zone

Self-care habits

Step 1. Understand the blue, red and green zones

Figures 9.2, 9.3 and 9.4 (overleaf) show examples of how other leaders think, feel and act when in each zone. Check through the items and then take a few minutes to create your own list.

How do you think...	How do you feel...	What do you do...
Strategic	Calm and composed	Take long-term view
Clear-minded	Alert	Connect the dots
Keep it simple	Confident	Create effective plans
Present and engaged	Optimistic	Listen attentively
Aware of people dynamics	Energetic	Build partnerships

Figure 9.2: leadership in the blue zone

REFLECT
Blue zone

Record your insights and reflections on the Self-care Canvas as you answer the following questions about your 'blue zone'.

» How does blue zone thinking impact your personal and leadership effectiveness?

» What do you do better when you are in the blue zone?

How do you think ...	How do you feel ...	What do you do ...
Cluttered mind	Impatient	Act impulsively
Win or lose	Edgy	Get aggressive with others
Fixed	Cynical	Dismiss alternative views

Figure 9.3: leadership in the red zone

REFLECT

Red zone

Record your insights and reflections on the Self-care Canvas as you answer the following 'red zone' questions.

» How does red zone thinking impact your effectiveness?

» What are the benefits and costs of red zone feelings and actions?

How do you think ...	How do you feel ...	What do you do ...
Distracted	Worrying	Procrastinate
What might happen	Doubting	Wait on others
Not making a mistake	Lethargic	Overthink/overprepare

Figure 9.4 leadership in the green zone

REFLECT

Green zone

Record your insights and reflections on the Self-care Canvas as you answer the 'green zone' questions.

» How does green zone thinking impact your effectiveness?

» What are the benefits and costs of green zone feelings and actions?

Step 2. Identify your A-game triggers and blockers

Triggering your blue zone isn't like the law of gravity: it doesn't always work. However, many of the *Toolkit for Turbulence* tools will help you to trigger it more often.

To find your primary triggers and blockers we recommend focusing on two broad aspects of the way you live, work and play. This will help you to make good choices on the sort of self-care and tactics to best set you up to consistently play your A-game.

Life pillars

Let's start with *life pillars*, and for those we turn to Stanford Neuroscience Professor Andrew Huberman and his 'Five Pillars of Health and Wellbeing': Sleep, Sunlight, Movement, Nutrients and Relationships (including with self). These five priorities seem incredibly obvious, but Huberman notes that often one or more pillars are out of shape. That's a recipe to go red or green. Following are brief descriptions of the five pillars.

Use the Self-care Canvas to capture your reflections and thoughts as you answer these questions.

PILLAR 1. SLEEP

Being well rested from regular high-quality sleep sets the tone for being more alert and high functioning during the day. *How do your sleep patterns help or hinder your mindset and therefore your effectiveness?*

PILLAR 2. SUNLIGHT

Sunlight gives your vitamin D levels a boost and releases dopamine, which makes you feel good and is beneficial for brain and body. *Are you enjoying enough sunlight, particularly early in the day? Is this a potential trigger or blocker?*

PILLAR 3. MOVEMENT

Any sort of movement for at least 20 minutes gives the body a boost of positive chemicals and blood flow. *How's your daily dose of movement? What do you know about your own body and how movement helps to trigger blue zone states?*

PILLAR 4. NUTRIENTS

Get to know what's healthy and what's not for your unique system, including foods and liquids. *Is this an area where you can boost your energy and wellbeing?*

PILLAR 5. RELATIONSHIPS (INCLUDING WITH SELF)

Constructive relationships are pivotal to wellbeing, so be sure to spend time with people who bring you energy and connection. *Which relationships and interpersonal practices are most important to finding your A-game? How does your relationship with yourself impact your zones?*

Performance practices

The second aspect connected to your A-game is what sport psychologists call 'performance practices'. These are the conditions or practices that typically trigger high-performance mind states, of which there are four that warrant deliberate attention.

Use the Self-care Canvas to capture your reflections and thoughts as you answer the following questions.

A big challenge	Meaningful purpose and goals
The challenge of a 'quest' lifts many people into their zone, although if the challenge is too big it can have the opposite effect.	A clear and meaningful purpose or goal is a likely trigger to your A-game.
» *Is there an inspiring 'mountain' to climb?* » *What challenges trigger blue zone for you?*	» *Are you clear on what matters?* » *Are goals important triggers for you?*
Clear mind	**Rituals and routines**
A clear mind isn't empty — it's focused on what matters most, and that's why so many athletes adopt a mindfulness practice.	A proven key to consistently finding the A-game is repeatable rituals and routines.
» *What helps or hinders you from bringing a clear and focused mind?* » *What does this suggest for future habits?*	» *What rituals and routines currently help you to find your A-game?* » *What new habit could lift your physical and mental energy?*

Step 3. Commit to self-care habits that trigger your zone

The 'zone' gives you a reference point to help you select self-care strategies to suit your own unique psychology. It also brings together performance and wellbeing in a practical way.

REFLECT
Start, stop, continue

Based on your reflections from the activities you have just worked through:

» *Are there things you might **START** or do more of to create those blue zone/A-game experiences?* For example, could you develop a better routine for exercise and sleep, give attention to nutrition or get better at defining real priorities?

» *Have you gained any insights on habits or practices that deplete energy or trigger an unhelpful mindset?* These are things to **STOP** doing or do less of, such as unhealthy lifestyle habits around drinking and sleep, or overcommitting at work or outside work in community activities.

» *What current practices help you to find and sustain the blue zone?* These are things to **CONTINUE** such as exercise, blocking time in your schedule for deep work and spending time with colleagues who stimulate your creativity.

Record these reflections on the Self-care Canvas and be sure to make these essential practices in your toolkit for turbulence.

Learnings

» **Performance and wellbeing** can't be sustained without prioritising self-care.

» It is common for the first casualty of increased turbulence at work or home to be **self-care**, so be aware of the need to prioritise this essential contributor to performance and wellbeing.

» **A-game** level is when you are clear minded, engaged fully in the task and open to opportunity. It is your natural **adaptive mindset**: *constructive – courageous – creative*.

» Things seem easier in the **blue zone**, and more difficult in the red and green zones.

» When you understand your blue, red and green zones it offers a simple and effective tool to help manage your own physical and mental **energy** levels.

» Be alert to your A-game **triggers and blockers** so you can manage them effectively every day.

» Commit to **self-care habits** that trigger your zone. They will lay the foundation for performance and wellbeing and help you to be a better person and leader.

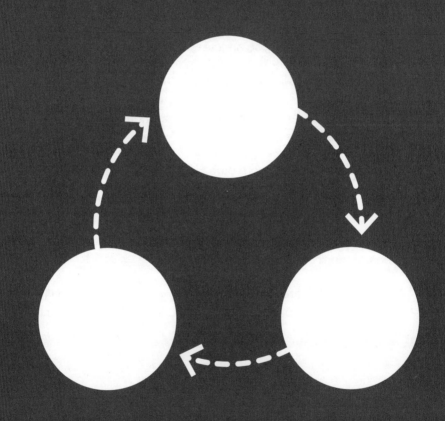

4

Team up

*... to align, collaborate and
learn together*

In Part 3 you learned about **recalibrating** the mindset that accompanies an advantage leader's approach to disruption. In the following four chapters we focus on your team by first introducing a **blueprint for teamwork,** which is laid out on a canvas for easy navigation. Then you will apply the blueprint as a learning loop to **align** your team's direction and focus, foster **collaboration** through connection and synergy, and accelerate **learning** through awareness and tempo. A host of **tools and examples** will guide you through this important section.

CHAPTER 10

A blueprint for teamwork

Do you view your team as one of your greatest assets? Are you keen to unlock the potential of your team as individuals and collectively? Is a high-performing team essential to your business strategy and personal aspirations?

If you've answered 'yes' to any of these questions, then these chapters are for you! They offer a step-by-step guide to transforming team culture and ways of working to suit the challenges of today and tomorrow. You will find chapters chockful of proven tools and techniques to supercharge your team to sustain performance and wellbeing in high-demand conditions.

A shared framework

The starting point for building a top team is a shared understanding of the essential characteristics or building blocks for a high-performing team. You need that so everyone is clear and aligned about what a top-performing team really is. The challenge is to make it compellingly practical, while not oversimplifying the complexities of team direction, dynamics and development.

In this part we offer a framework to describe, create and evaluate the way your team, or any team, is set up and how it operates. That framework is in the form of a learning loop model that has been applied and proven as part of the Think One Team method (www.thinkoneteam.com) in a wide array of enterprises and government settings ranging from start-ups to the executive teams of multinational corporations. It has also been used to support agile implementations, to fast-track the development of cross-functional tiger teams and to guide the forming, building, and reimagining of countless departmental and divisional teams.

The framework gives you a simple shared language to collaborate with your team and other leadership colleagues to create the optimal operating rhythm, tools and practices. It also provides a baseline for assumptions to be continually challenged and refined — something that is increasingly important in turbulence.

Without a framework, teamwork can be a mystery, or a jumble of important but disconnected ideas like trust, purpose, dynamics and collaboration.

Three core elements

Observe any team operating effectively at pace in a high-demand environment and at the heart of their ability to deliver consistent high performance will be a loop of three core activities: *Alignment, Collaboration* and *Learning*.

You can use these three elements, called ACL, to shape your team framework and identify the building blocks for any team. When unpacked the team framework offers a blueprint to guide the conversations about team plans, processes and practices. Here are those elements and a powerful set of associated questions.

Align

To be aligned is to commit to shared direction and focus.

> » What is our purpose and vision for success?

> » What are our goals and priorities?

> » What values and behaviours are important to guide our actions?

Without a shared understanding and commitment to these elements, team members lack unity, engagement and the will to collaborate and learn.

Collaborate

To collaborate is to share in a spirit of working as one.

» How strong is our trust and commitment to each other?

» Are we leveraging resources by co-creating and tackling problems together?

» Is our decision making and execution coordinated?

Without sharing there is inevitably waste, missed opportunities, disengagement, and the risks that come from silos and poorly executed strategies.

Learn

To learn is to be open, agile and adaptable (for a purpose).

» Are we open to learn from feedback, being challenged and reflection?

» Are we empowered, accountable and adding value?

» What's our optimal operating rhythm?

Without adaptability built into your operating rhythm the team will be too slow to respond in the face of rapid and unpredictable change.

Operating rhythm

While the ACL elements can be described separately, the secret to success is to understand how they interact with one another to create cycles of alignment, collaboration and learning (see figure 10.1, overleaf).

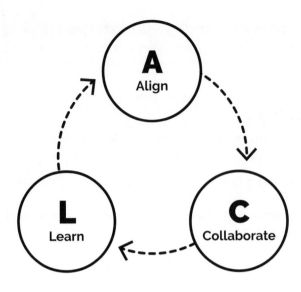

Aligning	Collaborating	Learning
Planning and budgeting	Meetings and forums	Monitoring and reviewing
Setting clear goals	Communicating	Renewing
Agreeing on expectations	Problem solving	Reporting
	Co-creating	Improving and adapting
Prioritising/ sequencing		

Figure 10.1: the ACL model

Operating rhythm is the pace and tempo of the rituals, routines and actions by which teams align, collaborate and learn. There is no right or wrong way, just the underlying principle of 'loop and learn' to navigate through changing context, in much the same way as a sailboat skipper and crew continually align, collaborate and learn.

Sometimes the operating rhythm is dictated by the context in which the team is operating. A basketball team has a game-day rhythm; an executive team reports in governance cycles. At other times the team defines its own tempo, such as weekly agile sprints or a 90-day performance cycle.

Paul Duldig reflects on the 90-day or quarterly operating rhythm at Australian National University. 'It has served us really well in crisis and as a way to get the tempo needed to deliver in more settled times. Teams set up and then it's quarterly targets and feedback around the right conversations.'

You'll find more detail and additional tools to help you develop your operating rhythm tempo, principles and practices in chapter 13. For now, just keep in mind that every tool interacts with every other tool in some way. The primary tool *Team Canvas* will show you how to pull them all together for your team.

Team Canvas

The basic Team Canvas illustrates the three core elements, *align*, *collaborate* and *learn*, then describes two essential building blocks for team effectiveness in each: *Direction and Focus, Connection and Synergy, Awareness and Tempo*.

Let's explore the tool.

Team Canvas

The Team Canvas provides the overall framework to evaluate the team setup and choose the optimal tools to sustain and grow team effectiveness.

OVERVIEW

The Team Canvas is your one-page guide to the key building blocks of high-performance teamwork.

You can evaluate your team's current strengths and needs for improvement against the elements on the Team Canvas. The following three chapters provide the tools needed to set up your team to align, collaborate and learn.

Team Canvas

Align

1 Direction

Clear and meaningful team purpose

Average:

Compelling vision and narrative to capture the hearts and minds of our people

Average:

2 Focus

Shared values/principles reflected in team member behaviours

Average:

Agreed priorities and goals for the right horizons

Average:

Collaborate

3 Connection

Healthy interpersonal trust amongst team members

Average:

Strong partnering relationships and practices

Average:

4 Synergy

Effective collaborative problem solving and co-creation

Average:

Synergistic decision making

Average:

Learn

5 Awareness

Openness to reflect, give and receive feedback and to challenge

Average:

Relentless debriefing

Average:

6 Tempo

Disciplined operating rhythm/performance cycle cadence

Average:

Delivering outcomes at pace through empowerment and accountability

Average:

How to use the Team Canvas

To fully set up your team we recommend a process covering five phases: *Evaluate, Envision, Assemble, Implement* and *Adapt*. Figure 10.2 summarises the aims of each phase.

Evaluate	Identify and quantify your team strengths and gaps.
Envision	Describe your optimal team setup and ways of working.
Assemble	Prioritise your team development needs and tools.
Implement	Weave tools and practices into your team operating rhythm.
Adapt	Adapt and modify the team practices in response to what's happening.

Figure 10.2: phases in deploying the Team Canvas

The progression through these phases isn't intended to be linear. Assembling and Implementation will likely be continuous while you Evaluate, Envision and Adapt.

For the best results we recommend starting with *Evaluate* and working through this phase personally and with your team.

We'll show how to use the Team Canvas to evaluate and set up the ways of working for your team. The following chapters then deep dive into *Align, Collaborate* and *Learn* to provide the tools you'll need to equip your team to navigate disruption and turn turbulence to advantage.

Phase 1. Evaluate

The aim of this phase is to identify and quantify team strengths and gaps so you can define development priorities for your team and affirm ways of working.

Here we describe an example of how the Team Canvas is used by a team. You can use the same process to conduct your own evaluation.

CASE EXAMPLE

A team from a human services enterprise used the Team Canvas to evaluate team strengths and gaps for the purpose of setting up for a new year.

Posted on the wall on their arrival was an A0-sized poster of the Team Canvas together with stacks of Post-it notes and sharpies. The facilitator explained how the Team Canvas framework was based on the ACL loop and pointed to the six building blocks, encouraging questions along the way.

The team worked through the canvas one building block at a time. Using a rating scale from –5 (significant derailer) to +5 (significant enabler), each individual was asked to rate the team against the two prompting items by placing Post-it notes with their rating in the appropriate spots.

The facilitator then used a large Post-it to show the average score for each item in that block (see example in figure 10.3, overleaf).

A brief discussion then followed to draw out reasons for the ratings in that block. The facilitator recorded those insights.

Over approximately 45 minutes the team rated and discussed each item until the Team Canvas provided a clear one-page view of the current maturity of the team in every area of the canvas.

The outcome of this activity was confirmation of three immediate priorities:

1. **Focus**. Define and align on priorities in 90-day cycles.

2. **Connection**. Strengthen partnering relationships and practices among team members.

3. **Tempo**. Tighten the operating rhythm to get greater visibility when things are off track.

Team Canvas

Average scores on evaluation

(A) Align

1 Direction

Clear and meaningful team purpose

Average: +2

Compelling vision and narrative to capture the hearts and minds of our people

Average: -1

2 Focus

Shared values/principles reflected in team member behaviours

Average: +3

Agreed priorities and goals for the right horizons

Average: -1

(C) Collaborate

3 Connection

Healthy interpersonal trust amongst team members

Average: +2

Strong partnering relationships and practices

Average: -1

4 Synergy

Effective collaborative problem solving and co-creation

Average: +3

Synergistic decision making

Average: +4

(L) Learn

5 Awareness

Openness to reflect, give and receive feedback and to challenge

Average: +3

Relentless debriefing

Average: +2

6 Tempo

Disciplined operating rhythm/performance cycle cadence

Average: -1

Delivering outcomes at pace through empowerment and accountability

Average: +4

Figure 10.3: Team Canvas evaluation

Apart from providing a clear sense of strengths and gaps, the Team Canvas evaluation is also an excellent team development activity because it encourages everyone to contribute equally and agree a shared path forward.

One important point to emphasise is that getting a +5 is quite an achievement and it is not expected that teams will want to reach that level on every item. For example, an average score of +3 for 'Clear and meaningful team purpose' could be quite adequate, whereas the team might aim closer to +5 on 'Healthy interpersonal trust'.

Phase 2. Envision

The aim of this phase is to describe the optimal team setup and ways of working. This can be beneficial particularly for new teams or consistency across multiple teams.

The process is straightforward and requires asking the team to debate and define what success will mean for each building block on the canvas. Once complete, it gives a clear framework for choosing tools, prioritising development activities and guiding overall team development.

For example, a defence enterprise has used the canvas for this purpose over several years to shape the development of team capabilities across the whole enterprise.

Figure 10.4 highlights some of the intentions they defined:

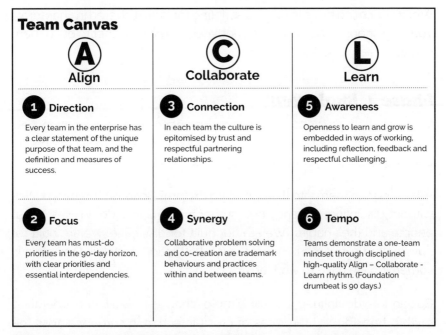

Figure 10.4: example of optimal setup for a team of teams

Phase 3. Assemble

This is the phase where you prioritise development needs and tools based on the insights gained from the earlier phases.

Those tools might be drawn from this book, your own playbooks or other sources. It is up to you to choose those that are most suited to your context and needs.

For example, to *align* your team you might choose to use a *Team Diamond* which is described in the next chapter. This is a great way to efficiently build commitment to the team purpose and high-level priorities.

If the need is to *collaborate*, you might choose to engage everyone in a shared tool like the *PROBED collaborative problem solving* tool in chapter 12.

When your mind turns to *learn*, debriefing tools are covered in chapter 13. You may choose to use them immediately or refine further to build them into your team operating rhythm.

Phase 4. Implement

Implementing your chosen tools and practices is about creating new habits that are integrated into the operating rhythm so they become an ongoing feature of your team's ways of working.

Why integrate them into the operating rhythm? Because they won't stick without discipline. As renowned surgeon Atul Gawande advises about people and their habits, 'We are not built for discipline. We are built for novelty and excitement, not for careful attention to detail. Discipline is something we have to work at.'

Gawande's disciplined use of simple checklists built into operating rhythm transformed the rates of cross-infection in surgery across the world, and his methods have been widely adopted to help professionals to work in disciplined and effective ways.

Phase 5. Adapt

An effective operating rhythm will ensure that you regularly monitor, evaluate and adapt your tools and practices based on what is happening to your team and enterprise.

In the continually changing environment you will inevitably be refining tools and adding new ways of working to adapt to changing conditions.

We recommend building regular reviews of team performance into your operating rhythm and sharing your Team Canvas whenever a new member joins. This will ensure that everyone is literally on the same page.

Before we move on

The most adaptable people and teams almost always have a repeatable cycle of alignment, collaboration and learning, which enables them to navigate flexibly through changeable conditions to achieve great outcomes.

This loop-and-learn approach is much like you'd see among the crew of a racing yacht, and is characteristic of all enterprises where small, agile teams are key to success, such as military special forces, Olympic sports, first responders and performing arts.

In a fast-changing and uncertain environment, the ability to *spin the ACL* is mission critical. You're now ready to move on and deep dive into the next three chapters, in order to:

- » align for total commitment

- » collaborate as one

- » make team learning a habit.

Learnings

» The starting point for teamwork is a **shared understanding** of the purpose and characteristics of a top team.

» Three activities, **alignment**, **collaboration** and **learning** (ACL), are core to the DNA of high-performing teams.

» The ACL describes the natural **learning loop** of top teams and comprises:

  » **Align.** Commit to a shared direction and focus.

  » **Collaborate**. Share in the spirit of working as one.

  » **Learn**. Be open, agile and adaptable.

» **Operating rhythm** is the pace and tempo of rituals, routines and actions by which teams align, collaborate and learn. There is no right or wrong rhythm, just the underlying principle of using loop and learn to navigate through a changing context.

» The **Team Canvas** unpacks the ACL into six building blocks that underpin a team development process comprising five phases: **Evaluate**, **Envision**, **Assemble**, **Implement** and **Adapt**.

» Start by completing the **evaluation exercise** on the Team Canvas and then work through the phases in a nonlinear way to suit your needs and the needs of your team and organisation.

CHAPTER 11

Align for total commitment

What is the core purpose of your team? What behaviours will 'make or break' team commitment and cohesion? What are your priorities? How can you create a vision that will capture the hearts and minds of your team?

We have observed and applied countless approaches to facilitating the alignment of leaders and teams. Amongst these are 'North Stars', 'True North' and even 'Moon Shots', together with the usual 'Mission – Vision – Values' frameworks.

Each of these has merit. However, we believe that alignment is achieved only when there is *commitment* to a shared direction and focus. Accordingly, the two building blocks in this chapter as defined on the Team Canvas are *Direction* and *Focus*.

You may choose just to go straight to the priorities that emerged in your Team Canvas evaluation activity, or work through the sequence as shown in the snapshot of the Align portion of the canvas.

Align

1 **Direction**

A Clear and meaningful team purpose

B Compelling vision and narrative to capture the hearts and minds of our people

2 **Focus**

A Shared values/principles reflected in team member behaviours

B Agreed priorities and goals for the right horizons

----

❶ Direction

To achieve strong team alignment, it's crucial to establish a clear purpose that ignites a shared sense of meaning. From there a compelling vision that paints an inspiring picture of the future will help you to engage your team, and gain wholehearted commitment to common goals.

Both, and

The Murray–Darling Basin is Australia's largest and best-known river system. It's spread over four states and covers over a million square kilometres, an area larger than the combined size of France and Germany. The Basin directly supports around 3.5 million people and produces more than one-third of Australia's food.

Culturally the Basin is iconic. Indigenous communities have a 50 000+ year connection that is fundamental to their identity and wellbeing. The Basin is a part of the national psyche and of the national economy, contributing over $30 billion annually from food production and tourism.

The ever-evolving Australian climate has seen the Basin face devastating droughts and floods, at times struggling to strike a balance between sustaining the health and wellbeing of the rivers and ground water, and supporting communities and industry. This has been a source of intense conflict between the states, the Commonwealth and disparate interest groups.

The Murray–Darling Basin Authority (MDBA) was created in 2008 to provide independent science-backed stewardship of the Basin and since its formation has operated the river system on behalf of the states and coordinated the overall Basin Plan.

Andrew McConville took over as CEO of the MDBA in 2022 and immediately grasped the complexity of the role played by his organisation.

'We had great work being done by skilled and committed people, but they were being pulled in many different directions. My role was to bring the direction and focus onto what mattered most, so we are set up to provide the best outcomes for all our stakeholders.'

In a previous role with Syngenta AG, an international provider of agricultural science and technology, Andrew had seen the positive benefits when people unite around a compelling core strategic narrative. He didn't want to outsource that, preferring instead to co-facilitate a series of staff conversations and design exercises, which led to a shared story, the *MDBA Way*.

In a succinct illustrated narrative, the *MDBA Way* captures the purpose, essential pillars of strategy and cornerstones of the culture. Andrew reflects, 'It's great when you see your team members genuinely excited and saying, "I can see why we exist and I love the ambition to be a part of the solution, not a part of the problem, and I can see where I fit in".'

The *MDBA Way* provides the essential framework for alignment of priorities. There's one other critical thread running through this work, however, and it is fundamental to leading through turbulence. That thread is *a paradox mindset*.

Paradox mindset

A 1996 study of Nobel laureates and famous scientists by Harvard University psychiatrist Albert Rothenberg revealed a core secret of revolutionary thinkers. He found they flipped conventional wisdom, which thought of things as either/or, right or wrong, and instead concentrated on what he called *multiple opposites simultaneously*. In other words, instead of either/or, right or wrong thinking, they adopted 'both, and' thinking. For Einstein this meant considering how an object can both move and rest at the same time, depending on the position of the observer. That breakthrough thinking led to his now famous theory of relativity.

Turbulence is full of paradoxes, such as those developed by a leadership team shown in figure 11.1. Evidence suggests that teams perform better when they uncover and talk about paradoxes instead of leaving them unspoken.

Act with clarity and certainty	*and*	Embrace and accept ambiguity
Deliver short-term outcomes	*and*	Create long-term value
Work as partners	*and*	Hold others to account
Be flexible and adaptive	*and*	Be disciplined
Protect from risks	*and*	Take calculated risks
Make unpopular decisions	*and*	Build trust
Uphold values	*and*	Make the trade-off decisions
Engage and consult openly	*and*	Act decisively at pace

Figure 11.1: examples of paradoxes

At MDBA, Andrew McConville and his team operate in one of the most complex environments imaginable, at the intersection of potential environmental, cultural, political and economic flashpoints. Turbulence can come from any and every direction, which is why the first leadership alignment activity MDBA undertook was a co-facilitated exercise, led by Andrew and Graham, that identified paradoxes such as:

» environmental water flows and water for industry and communities

» taking a whole-of-basin perspective and being responsive to local needs and interests.

Both situations need to be addressed by a *paradox mindset*. For example, the challenge is not to decide whether to deliver more water to the environment or to industry and communities, but rather to creatively hold the tension between both needs and to explore and find different ways to meet the core needs.

Can you recognise paradoxes where 'both, and' thinking might be required?

The primary tool *Beautiful paradoxes* will help your team to explore how to identify and manage paradoxes, which is excellent preparation for the Direction and Focus tools that follow.

PRIMARY TOOL
Beautiful paradoxes

Teams do better when paradoxes are surfaced and talked about. This normalises uncertainty, helps to build confidence and creativity, and reduces the likelihood of triggering defensive behaviours during alignment activities. This tool will help guide that process.

INSTRUCTIONS

1. Invite your team to participate in an activity where they will discuss the implications of paradoxes for planning, prioritising and decision making.

2. Present the following structure on a slide, whiteboard or handout (insert your own examples), and ask people to individually jot down examples of paradoxes that come to mind for them. Highlight that there are no right or wrong answers.

The challenge is to do this ...	and, at the same time, to do this
Example. Lead high-priority projects at scale and manage to meet tight deadlines.	**Example.** Keep multiple stakeholders engaged to enable the buy-in needed for successful delivery.

3. Share a personal story of a time when you struggled to 'hold the tension' so people can see this is something 'safe' to discuss in a group environment. Break into small groups for people to share their paradoxes and their associated feelings about them. Ask the groups to capture key thoughts.

4. Ask each subgroup to share two or three paradoxes that seemed to generate the most energy in the discussion. Use this opportunity to introduce the language of the *paradox mindset* (holding the tension and working with *both, and*).

5. Collate the paradoxes so they can be used in the alignment activities and close off with a reminder that strengthening the paradox mindset helps to cope with complexity and volatility.

Choosing the team direction

Of all the paradoxes confronting leaders, one of the most significant is the need to make choices about strategic direction while at the same time facing an environment of almost constant change.

Rebecca James, Group CEO of **humm**group, describes this dilemma: 'In a leadership role you have this real urge to make promises and commitments about the future because you think that is settling for people. However, you have to resist the urge to do it in such a rapidly changing macroeconomic environment.'

How do you set direction in that type of environment? What is helpful, what is a hindrance and what is even a complete waste of time?

Tanya Monro reminds us that the choices around direction and priorities mean 'always deeply reflecting on and honing your ability to see which battles matter in the longer arc of leadership. And to build that awareness in your team as well.'

We agree. It requires real clarity about the purpose of the team and the longer term direction.

The two items on the Team Canvas are the guide for what follows:

A.   Clear and meaningful team purpose

B.   Compelling vision and narrative to capture hearts and minds.

Item A. Team purpose

It is amazing how many teams struggle to clearly define their purpose. Some just haven't given thought to why they exist, beyond being a convenient collection of functions and roles. Sadly, most tend to use their to-do list as a default definition of purpose. For example, a corporate services team defines their purpose as 'delivering effective services to the wider enterprise', while a sales team points to 'achieving sales and revenue targets'.

There's no question that these are indicators of success, but are they really the core reason why the team itself exists? This is a very narrow, task-oriented way to define team purpose and risks missing potential a team can unlock.

Having a clear purpose will help your team forge a clear and compelling sense of identity and intent. This in turn will make it easier to stay focused on the things that matter most and will be particularly useful when choosing priorities and setting boundaries.

Let's use some tools to get the clarity and alignment you need.

Co-creating the team purpose

One of our favourite TEDx talks is *How to Know Your Life Purpose in Five Minutes* by film producer and popular speaker Adam Leipzig.

In a relaxed and engaging presentation, Leipzig proposes five simple questions to guide you towards discovering your life purpose. The magic of his approach is to lift people's thinking from describing what they do to how other people change or transform as a result of what they do. For example, instead of a teacher describing their purpose as 'I teach maths and science to secondary school students' (which is what they do), they might say, 'I show young people how to stretch their minds so they become lifelong learners and problem solvers' (which describes a more compelling purpose behind what they do).

This approach can light up a room as people see beyond their 'I teach' mindset and realise they 'stretch minds'.

The concept behind this approach is very similar to the sales process of converting features into benefits, so we took our inspiration from Leipzig and from the sales benefits approach to craft five questions to help teams to look beyond the features of what they do and to see a purpose in the benefits they offer to others.

This approach is captured in the primary tool *Co-creating the team purpose*. We recommend doing this before the following primary tool, *Team Diamond*, because it helps to open up the creativity of the team.

Co-creating the team purpose

This tool describes a facilitated process to help your team to co-create a succinct and meaningful team purpose.

INSTRUCTIONS

1. Before gathering your team together, ask them to watch the Adam Leipzig TEDx clip and complete the 'How to know your life purpose in five minutes' exercise for themselves.

2. Gather your people and begin by asking if they are open to sharing the outputs from the exercise with one or two colleagues. After a few minutes in small groups ask for volunteers to share with the whole group. Use this to highlight the magic in switching from 'what we do' thinking to 'how others change or transform' thinking.

3. Walk through the five team questions shown overleaf and have each individual jot down their own thoughts before sharing to optimise personal involvement and creativity.

4. As a group, step through each question, drawing out the common and interesting words, phrases and themes. Be sure to get everyone's input and discuss as much as required to get commitment to a draft of key words and phrases for each question.

5. Aim to get commitment to the main points, and expect and welcome some challenging and constructive conflict. Then ask for a subgroup to take your draft and refine it further prior to your next team development session. Some teams get this down to one sentence, while others develop a longer narrative. Overleaf is an example of a finished product.

Example of team purpose

> We are ABC Team. We inspire, we lead, we coach and we live the ABC values. We do it for our customers, people, and the communities with whom we engage. They look to us for clarity of purpose and direction, success, care and connection. Because we do this well, they are proud to be part of ABC as they realise their aspirations and reinforce the ABC values and core purpose.

Team questions

» What is the name of our team?

» What do we do collectively?

» Who do we do this for?

» What do these people or entities want or expect from us?

» How do they change or transform as a result of what we do as a team?

Team Diamond

Would you like a 'go-to' tool that has proven itself time and again as effective in gaining alignment within leadership teams? The approach is quick and simple, and we have seen it unite high-powered teams (even those that are deeply fractured) across sectors and enterprises as diverse as banking, defence, software, human services, utilities and universities.

The primary tool *Team Diamond* is underpinned by a favourite method of sports coaches, *constraints*.

In sport, a skilled coach will construct training conditions with intentional limits (constraints) on space, time and other factors to create pressure. For example, soccer players are drilled in tightly defined spaces with extra opponents to hone their protection and passing skills under pressure. The constraints add psychological pressure to the training, providing a type of 'forcing function', which stimulates creative problem solving.

The Team Diamond tool is also designed with intentional constraints on space and time. This will be helpful in shaping your team's focus and energy on finding a practical and pragmatic solution to the often mind-numbingly tedious process of defining team purpose and high-level priorities. (If possible, do the primary tool *Co-creating the team purpose* before this activity.)

Team Diamond

The Team Diamond will help cut through complexity and guide your team to confirming their purpose and high-level priorities. It will also allow you to describe them to others in a compelling and effective way.

INSTRUCTIONS

1. Confirm that the objective of the session is to draft and commit to *team purpose* and to define high-level priorities and expected success indicators.

2. Refer to the three guiding questions shown on the next page and show them on a screen or whiteboard to guide the activity.

3. Show the team the Team Diamond example and agree on time constraints (45–60 minutes) for initial drafting of the Diamond. If you have a largish team, consider breaking into subgroups to draft. Don't strive for 'perfection'; rather, agree on a draft Diamond and then how best to refine it.

4. After drafting the Diamond, seek agreement that a subgroup of the whole team will work on refining the draft Diamond ready for further discussion and sign-off at the next meeting.

5. Next, consider and agree on who should evaluate your team performance against the purpose and areas of focus. Ask the follow-on question, 'How would they rate our team performance against our Diamond today?' This can be quite confronting and generate lively conversation.

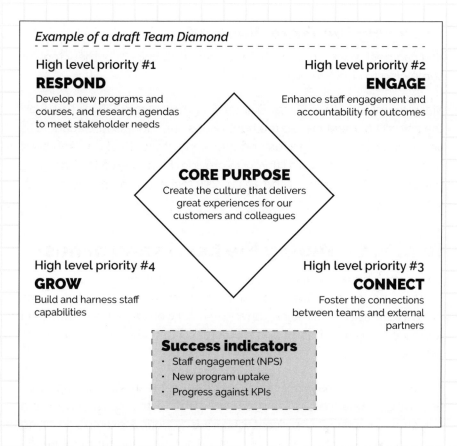

Example of a draft Team Diamond

High level priority #1
RESPOND
Develop new programs and
courses, and research agendas
to meet stakeholder needs

High level priority #2
ENGAGE
Enhance staff engagement and
accountability for outcomes

CORE PURPOSE
Create the culture that delivers
great experiences for our
customers and colleagues

High level priority #4
GROW
Build and harness staff
capabilities

High level priority #3
CONNECT
Foster the connections
between teams and external
partners

Success indicators
- Staff engagement (NPS)
- New program uptake
- Progress against KPIs

Guiding questions (on screen)

» If we were to create a Diamond to communicate to important
stakeholders, what is the single definition of team purpose we
would put in the middle?

» What are the four essential high-priority areas of focus for us as
a team to fulfil our purpose and achieve success?

» How will we know we've been 'successful' (measures or
indicators)?

Deploying the Team Diamond

You can decide whether the Team Diamond remains a primary tool, or something to check in on occasionally.

Many teams use their Team Diamond in three ways. Firstly to shape the agenda of meetings so the right issues are addressed. Secondly to share with other teams to foster better understanding of one another's direction and priorities, and thirdly to provide the framework for defining the specific deliverables the team will focus on in the next cycle (say, 90 days).

Item B. Capturing the hearts and minds

This is not a book about developing business strategy and plans, so we don't intend to deep dive into vision and mission. Nonetheless, teams need a narrative about their vision and ways of working to boost cohesion and to capture the hearts and minds of others who are important to achieving that vision.

For leadership teams this is critical, and for other teams it is an important way to generate passion and commitment to the cause. Too often the strategic planning process becomes a boring exercise in filling out a business template, rather than something that captures hearts and minds.

That's why we developed the primary tool *Hearts and minds narrative* and the accompanying Narrative Canvas as a shortcut to capturing those hearts and minds by creating a compelling story. The canvas is extremely effective and fun to complete. Use it with your team to shape and clarify the vision or to prepare a 'pitch' that engages an audience (for example, staff or stakeholders).

The canvas begins by clarifying the purpose of your narrative, the target audience and the outcomes you hope to achieve from telling this story.

From there you develop the most important narrative elements to create a powerful story incorporating a backstory with villains, a quest and a call to action.

Hearts and minds narrative

The tool uses the Narrative Canvas as a one-page template to help you create a compelling narrative of your team's vision. It must pass three tests: it must be *logical*, *believable* and *compelling*.

INSTRUCTIONS

1. Print or draw the Narrative Canvas (overleaf) and follow the questions and prompts on the following pages:

   Readying — defining why you are telling the story and to whom

   Backstory — important background and context

   Purpose and position — your purpose and how to connect with your audience

   Villains — the harsh realities

   Quest — your vision and plan

   Call to action — turning the talk into the walk.

   Be mindful that each section of the canvas is an activity in its own right and may require research, ideation and effective debate to hone the story into a compelling narrative.

2. When you have drafted your narrative it will be time to consider how best to present it to your audience. This is commonly done through websites, short videos, booklets or presentations at meetings and forums. Even if the intent of your narrative is simply to unite your team, it is still important to create a finished product for alignment and to be revisited as and when required.

Narrative Canvas

1 Readying

Why tell this story?

Who is the audience?

What does a 'successful pitch' mean?

2 Backstory

What history is important?

What content needs to be included?

What style of pitch will resonate best?

3 Purpose and position

How do we describe our core purpose?

How do we show credibility?

What will demonstrate our empathy?

4 Villains

What are the harsh realities?

What or who is the main villain?

Why is it wrong for the villain(s) to prevail?

5 Quest

What's our inspiring picture of the future?

Why is it compelling?

What are the top moves to get there?

6 Call to action

What must happen to move forward?

What are the immediate actions?

Reminder ... why tell the story?

Narrative Canvas steps

1. Readying

Every narrative needs a clear purpose, a well-defined audience, and a clear and agreed view of what constitutes a 'successful pitch'. For example, we might use the canvas to tell the story of the need for a toolkit for turbulence. Our audience might be a group of business leaders, and a successful pitch judged by people wanting to read the book and apply the tools. When creating your narrative be prepared to create 'customised' versions for different audiences.

Key prompts

- » Why tell this story?
- » Who is the audience?
- » What does a 'successful pitch' mean for each audience?

2. Backstory

This is about building a coherent story, so the backstory needs to be logical and to connect the past to your ultimate vision. Explaining the history and current context is an important part of creating a logical, believable and compelling narrative.

Key prompts

- » What history is important?
- » What context needs to be included?
- » What style of pitch will resonate best?

3. Purpose and position

This is about describing the purpose in a way that ensures people know who you are and why you are about to pitch a 'quest'. It's also important to consider how you can position this to engage your audience and establish credibility — for example, you might highlight past experience and include data that supports your case. Be sure to show empathy for your audience by demonstrating that you understand their position, and acknowledge any stress or frustrations they are experiencing.

Key prompts

- » How do we describe our core purpose?
- » How do we show credibility?
- » What words or actions will help to demonstrate our empathy?

4. Villains

The harsh realities that stand in the way of success need to be named, because part of a compelling story is to take on and defeat the villains.

Key prompts

- » What are the harsh realities?
- » What or who is the main villain?
- » Why is it wrong for the villain(s) to prevail?

5. Quest

This is the centrepiece of your pitch and includes a vision of success, compelling reasons why success matters, and the big 'moves' that demonstrate you are serious, and that you can and will succeed.

Key prompts

- » What's our inspiring picture of the future?
- » Why is the quest compelling to the audience?
- » What are the big moves to get there?

6. Call to action

Every narrative needs a call to action to turn the *talk* into the *walk*. Here it is important to consider what you are asking of people and how to secure their commitment. Be sure to revisit the imperative, including contrasting what success means with what failure would look like. Weaving the positives from success with the negatives of failure into your call to action will help to galvanise support.

Key prompts

- » What must happen before we can move forward?
- » What are our immediate actions?
- » Why is this story being told (a reminder)?

Recap

Creating a narrative is a great way to inspire and motivate team members and to build team identity and culture. The completed narrative itself will also provide a valuable tool to enable effective communication with stakeholders and help to get people involved and excited about your future and the part they can play. Give it the time and attention it deserves.

BUILDING BLOCK

2 Focus

With the foundation of *Team Direction* in place it's time for the rubber to hit the road by establishing the *Team Focus* to ensure the all-important clarity, accountability and trust.

The two items on the Team Canvas are the guide for what follows:

A. *team commitments (behaviours)* — agreeing your team's standards of behaviour

B. *team deliverables* — building the habit of delivering at pace.

We include team commitments in the canvas area of Focus because it is best to have the overall direction in place before having a serious conversation about the standards people expect of each other (but just prior to committing to deliverables).

In a nonlinear environment there really is no separation between planning and the development of team culture, because it is about adaptability rather than conventional business planning cycles and methods.

Rebecca James highlights how the commitment to team culture integrates with a dynamic approach to direction and focus at **humm**group: 'If you try to make promises to traditional cycles, like three-year plans, you set your business up for rigidity when what's needed is adaptability. Our direction is defined by our business model and our culture, and from there it's about adaptive forecasting, working to quarterly cycles, and great communication with all our people on a weekly cadence so people know the direction and what to focus on.'

Item A. Team commitments (behaviours)

Most high-performing teams have an implicit or explicit commitment to 'signature' or 'trademark' behaviours, so if you don't have clearly defined team behaviour standards, we recommend scheduling a team commitments conversation with your team.

Establishing these team standards is an important step in *team norming*, and there are a wide range of approaches to this activity. Ideally, however, it is done in an offsite or away-from-work location where people have time to reflect on what they want, need and expect from the team.

The primary tool *Team commitments (behaviours)* is your guide for this activity and includes an example of commitments developed with a leadership team. This describes the standards team members expect of one another and should be regularly reviewed and refined to suit the stage of development of the team or when a new team member joins.

Team commitments (behaviours)

Team commitments (behaviours) is an opportunity for the team to come together in a psychologically safe environment to raise, discuss and decide on team standards of behaviour.

INSTRUCTIONS

1. Gather your team together (face to face if possible) and begin by sharing that the aim of the session is to define and agree on a set of team commitments.

2. Use the Team Commitments example on the following page to describe the expected product of this activity.

3. Share the list of **Guiding Principles** (overleaf) for the conversation or develop your own with the team.

4. Step through the three Team Facilitation checkpoints:

   » **Checkpoint 1.** Team strengths and gaps

   » **Checkpoint 2.** Align to organisational values

   » **Checkpoint 3.** Refine and fine-tune commitments.

5. When the commitments are refined connect them to your operating rhythm to ensure regular reflection, learning and improvement. The reality of any list of team behaviours is the adage 'What you walk past you condone'. That's why the team commitments need to be regularly reviewed as part of the debriefing methods and tools covered in chapter 13.

Team Commitment resources and activities

Team Commitments example

Run through this Team Commitments example with your team.

> Our Team Commitments
>
> We each commit to the highest standards in these behaviours:
>
> **BE UNCOMFORTABLE; BE VULNERABLE —** Create and take the conversation where we need to go to break through.
>
> **BE A TRUSTED PARTNER —** Go direct, zero surprises, never undermine colleagues in words or actions.
>
> **BE CLEAR —** Confirm we always know and are fully committed to the next steps, relentlessly prioritise and debrief.
>
> **BE ACCOUNTABLE —** Own the outcome and the impacts of anything that affects the outcome.

Guiding principles

» **Be clear and specific** in describing actual behaviours (not just attitudes or intentions).

» **Choose behaviours** that, while not necessarily 'comfortable', will have the most impact.

» **Focus on leveraging** strengths and minimising the risks of derailers.

» **Limit the final commitments** to a maximum of five.

» **Document and sign off** on them to nail each commitment.

» **Regularly debrief** and seek feedback on how the team is living these commitments.

Team facilitation checkpoints

These are the three checkpoints for the *team commitments (behaviours)* activity.

Checkpoint 1. Team strengths and gaps

Guide the team through a discussion about strengths, gaps and needs. The following prompts may help to stimulate thinking and discussion:

- » Where are our strengths as a team (e.g. strategic thinking)?
- » Do we have 'strengths overplayed' (e.g. too much focus on detail)?
- » Do we have 'gaps' in team styles (e.g. too many idea generators and not enough completers)?
- » What behaviours will have the most impact on playing as a strong team (e.g. openness and sharing)?

We prefer to supplement this activity with data and insights from team profiles or similar instruments. The combination of self-awareness and sharing of team styles via a common framework and language can be very useful. Our preferred foundation inventory is from the Team Management Systems suite.

Checkpoint 2. Align to organisational values

Chances are you have published organisational values and/or behaviours, so take a few minutes to discuss and explore what they mean for your team behaviours. Consider if any of these need to be explicitly stated in your team commitments.

Checkpoint 3. Refine and fine-tune commitments

Use the insights from the discussions to draft a list of behaviours that team members feel are most important. This is usually best done via a Post-it note method so everyone's voice is heard. Sort into an initial set of behaviours.

Remind the team that most teams have agreed behaviours, while high-performing teams turn these into signature or trademark behaviours.

Encourage reflection and challenge to really home in on items that meet three tests:

- » essential to team performance
- » clear and concise in meaning
- » strong commitment from all members.

Finalise the commitments into 'Headlines' and 'Behaviours'. The example in the tool illustrates how the team developed a compelling headline for each item (for example, *Be uncomfortable; Be vulnerable*) and descriptive behaviours (for example, *Create and take the conversation where we need to go to break through*).

Recap

Candid conversations build trust among colleagues, particularly when they are about behaviours and standards. They also establish essential alignment about expectations and lay the foundation for team trademark behaviours that send a strong signal to others about the integrity and effectiveness of the team.

Item B. Team deliverables

What do you think is the most powerful psychological tool to deploy in a high-demand setting? Of course, there is no right answer to this question, but time and again the tool that proves most useful is the short-term goal.

Building the habit of delivering at pace

Emergency-room doctors and nurses use short-term goals to cut through the myriad demands pulling at their attention and emotions. Navy Seals training emphasises the power of micro-goals to get through impossibly tough challenges, and relay runners segment their races into sub-goals to optimise baton changes and race tactics. Short-term goals prove their value time and again.

If you have established your Team Diamond, then you are in a good place to break down your major priorities into short-term goals ('micro-deliverables') to answer the key question:

> » As a team, what deliverables will we hold ourselves to account for?

Let's unpack that question to set your team up to cut through and achieve great outcomes.

Accountability

The word 'accountability' gets tossed around a lot in business yet it is often poorly defined.

Imagine you are the skipper of a yacht. What does accountability mean in that context? It's quite simple, isn't it? As skipper you are responsible for everything associated with the boat, including safety, resources, crew roles, navigation and communication. Yes, the skipper is accountable, full stop.

Unfortunately, two things can disrupt that thinking when it is applied to the workplace. Firstly, some folks will balk at the idea that someone can be accountable for things they can't control. Fair point, and quite reasonable that a skipper isn't accountable for the weather, but when they take out the boat, they are accountable for the consequences, no matter if the weather forecast is wrong and the unexpected happens. The second thing is blame and shame, and that's mostly why people duck for cover when the uncontrollable upends things.

Individual accountability means you own it, and all the consequences; it is a cornerstone of trust.

Team accountability is a little less easy to define because it is the combination of team standards of behaviour, like acting on commitments and meeting the overall goals (see figure 11.2, overleaf). Again, a metaphor can be helpful. Imagine your team has mounted an Everest expedition. Two aspects of team accountability are key. First is that everyone commits to the mission to get one or more climbers to the summit and back again safely. Second is the ownership of team commitments, which means actively supporting and challenging each other on how these commitments are demonstrated. If someone is struggling, the team supports and/or challenges them; if there is a significant problem, they huddle around it. Team accountability is taking joint ownership to mobilise the resources of the team to achieve the mission.

Deliverables

A high-performing team delivers outcomes. It's not just about completed projects and achieving annual targets, however. In fact, it's less about end results and more about the team habit of committing to and achieving short-term goals, sometimes called micro-deliverables.

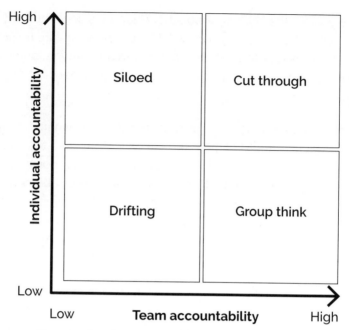

Figure 11.2: the magic of accountability

You need to build a team culture of accountability and confidence to consistently deliver outcomes, and to do that a team must have trust in the process and in each other.

How? Clarity about the team micro-deliverables and an agreed cadence (ACL).

Care Connect used the notion of a 90-day cycle to bring individual and team accountability together using a set of micro-deliverables. Care Connect CEO Paul Ostrowski notes: 'Inside every 90-day cycle we have approximately five focus priorities. Each of these has a clear 90-day deliverable and is owned by one of the Executive Team. We use our meetings and day-to-day partnering to support and challenge each other to achieve the milestones in the 90 days. These micro-deliverables have been extremely valuable in boosting our ability as a team to focus and collaborate under pressure, and they've lifted confidence because we see progress and achievement.'

The primary tool *90-day team deliverables* is a straightforward way for the team to use the power of short-term goals to establish accountability and focus.

It requires the team to set a time horizon (default 90 days) and agree on the most important things to deliver in that horizon. This will include individual accountability and alignment of expectations.

In preparing to facilitate the use of the tool make sure you are ready to clearly state your position on:

» the importance of short-term goals/deliverables to provide team focus and confidence

» definitions of and expectations of individual and team accountability

» a 90-day or equivalent cycle with a smallish set of team deliverables with individual accountabilities.

A set of clearly defined 90-day deliverables or equivalent will help to optimise outcomes and ensure the workloads and pace are sustainable by providing focus and empowerment.

Let's have a look at the primary tool *90-day team deliverables* and the accompanying canvas

90-day team deliverables

The *90-day team deliverables* tool defines the important team outcomes for the next performance cycle. Use it with the Team Diamond to ensure team focus.

INSTRUCTIONS

1. Open by confirming the key elements already noted including principles to help define the team deliverables (such as the impact on overall results).

2. Give each person 15 minutes and Post-it notes to answer the question:

   » What are the top five to seven deliverables we should focus on as a team in the next 90 days?

3. Use a suitable sorting process. For most teams, five to seven items is about the right balance of focus and spread. Allocate an accountable person for each deliverable.

4. Ask each accountable person to draft an initial scope for the deliverable using the Deliverable Canvas. This will require time to prepare and is usually part of a subsequent team session.

5. In that next session guide the conversation to ensure the team is aligned about the expectations for each deliverable, including what resources and other support will be needed to land it successfully.

Deliverable Canvas

	Name of team deliverable	Accountable person

Purpose What is the core purpose of this initiative?

Perfect Outcome What will 'done' look like at 90 days?

Principles What guidelines or principles are important?

Plan What is the high-level plan — defined in the 3Ws below?

What	By who	By when

Actioning the deliverables

You may find some team members are uncomfortable that initiatives don't fit neatly into 90 days. Acknowledge that the concerns about timeframes are completely understandable; however, this will be an issue irrespective of timescales.

The two keys to the ongoing success of 90-day deliverables are the cadence of tracking progress and the way your team works together to unlock potential and unblock where things are stuck or slow. A visual tracking system showing progress and current or potential blocks can be very helpful to support this process.

Learnings

» **Commitment** is at the heart of team alignment, because without it team members will lack the personal investment needed to work together through adversity towards shared goals and with a common purpose.

» Teams perform better when they uncover and talk about **paradoxes** instead of leaving them unspoken.

» A clear and compelling **team purpose** makes it easier to stay focused on the things that matter most and is particularly useful when choosing priorities and setting boundaries.

» The **Team Diamond** helps teams create the essential alignment about team purpose and priorities.

» A strong narrative about your team vision and ways of working will help to boost cohesion and to capture the hearts and minds of others who are important to achieving that vision. The **Narrative Canvas** shows you how to create a compelling narrative of the vision/quest that passes three tests: it's *logical, believable* and *compelling*.

» Create the opportunity for your team to come together in a psychologically safe environment to raise, discuss and decide on their team standards of behaviour. These will become the **team commitments**.

» *90-day team deliverables* is a process to use the power of short-term goals to help the team establish accountability and focus. This helps to optimise outcomes and ensure the workloads and pace are sustainable.

CHAPTER 12

Collaborate as one

How does team trust and unity develop? What tools inspire people to come together to solve their most challenging problems? What's the secret to getting things done across business unit boundaries and silos? How do you avoid disconnects that create bottlenecks, duplication and inefficiency?

To *collaborate* is to share in a spirit of working as one, because without sharing there is inevitably waste, missed opportunities, disengagement and the risks that come from silos and poorly executed strategies.

Working as one requires connection and synergy. Connection means healthy interpersonal trust among team members and strong partnering relationships, which are important to working in the churn of complexity. Synergy means the team leverages all its resources, collaborates effectively and makes good decisions.

This chapter is structured from those two building blocks, *connection* and *synergy*, and again each is divided into A and B elements, as shown in the snapshot of the Team Canvas.

As with the previous chapter, you may choose to work through from the start or go straight to an item you identified from your Team Canvas evaluation.

Collaborate

3 **Connection**

A Healthy interpersonal trust amongst team members

B Strong partnering relationships and practices

4 **Synergy**

A Effective collaborative problem solving and co-creation

B Synergistic decision making

3 Connection

Embedded within the essence of human nature, there is an inherent desire for meaningful interpersonal connections. Harnessing the immense power of this need for connection is your obligation and opportunity as a leader so that individuals are intricately linked to meet challenges as one united and connected team.

One team

For over a decade at the helm of the Australian Grand Prix Corporation (AGPC), Andrew Westacott had a bird's eye view of what he called 'the precision' of the world's top motorsport teams — Red Bull, Ferrari, Mercedes — and the relentless search for improvement and the winning edge. He treated his leadership of the AGPC with the same approach. 'Well, are we going to be Red Bull, or are we going to be in the middle or at the back of the pack?' he asked, challenging himself and his team to take on the world's best.

It's hard enough to stay at the front when everything is flowing, but how did Andrew keep his team motivated, connected and continuing to innovate when not just one race year was cancelled but two? Add to that the extended lockdowns in Victoria, which saw the world opening up while Melbourne didn't.

His answer wasn't motivation. It was collaboration and an inspiring initiative called 'Ready to Race'.

Andrew explains: 'We had to have everyone working as one team to deliver right up until cancellation and we needed to be world-class ready for whenever it did open back up. We couldn't be caught out saying, We haven't sold enough tickets, I haven't got a grandstand contract, the facilities haven't been designed and so on.

'So we created Ready to Race with over half a dozen teams championing work streams like circuit design, facility upgrades, fan experience, government regulations and approvals, and stakeholder engagement with Formula 1®. Everyone had a cross-functional involvement in a work stream of Ready to Race, and it gave that sense of shared purpose and involvement across the organisation which is essential to work as one team.

'We became more flexible and adaptable, and by 2022, when Australia reopened, the whole AGPC team was not only ready to race, but ready to race better than we had before and in a vastly changed world.'

The spirit of sharing

Collaboration means sharing in the spirit of working as one, and like the AGPC experience, it is crucial for everyone to have a clear and shared understanding of what working as one team actually means.

To work as one, a team needs five core characteristics demonstrated through behaviours and practices. These five characteristics were first described in Graham's *Think One Team* as the 'Five Shares': share the big picture, share the reality, share the air, share the load, and share the wins and losses.

Each 'share' has a 'shadow' associated with disunity, silos and protective behaviour. The five shares and their opposites were identified from studying the crucial practices that determined success or failure in cross-functional teams, including project and multilevel teams. Figure 12.1 (overleaf) highlights the core elements.

Getting to know the five shares

Understanding the strengths and weaknesses of your team against each of the five shares is a powerful step in creating the optimal environment to foster collaboration. To do that we explain each of the five shares with specific examples of behaviours and then pull those together into a primary tool, *Five shares (above the line/below the line)*, to evaluate your team and improve team effectiveness.

One Team	Disunity
Share the big picture	Pursue other agendas
Share the reality	Avoid and deny
Share the air	Stifle communication
Share the load	Look after your own turf
Share the wins and losses	Play I win, you lose

Figure 12.1: Think One Team Five Shares model

Share the big picture

Share the big picture ensures everyone understands and commits to playing their part in something bigger than their own goals and tasks. It happens because people can see the compelling 'why' behind decisions and understand how their actions affect the overall success of the team, project and/or enterprise. Leaders foster a 'share the big picture' mindset by aligning to purpose, cause or vision and by ensuring context is understood, such as the big threats and opportunities.

The shadow, *pursue other agendas*, happens when people or business units pursue other activities that they believe are more important than the big picture. Countless organisations experience this through internal competition, leaders who hoard information and resources, and the dreaded silos. Unfortunately, the reality is that *pursue other agendas* is reinforced through poorly designed incentives and outdated or disconnected systems, which slow down communication and limit understanding of the end-to-end process.

The more turbulence, the more important it is to ensure that people understand why the big picture matters, the context and their part in making it happen.

Share the reality

Share the reality is about being open, honest and straightforward in a way that builds trust and confidence. Teams that share the reality commit to transparency. They get issues out on the table, confront harsh realities and openly seek, receive and offer insights and feedback.

The shadow is *avoid and deny*, which is all about protective and defensive behaviours. It shows up in people putting an overly positive 'spin' on issues or avoiding them altogether. When reality is avoided or denied the whole organisation is at risk.

Share the air

Share the air is all about open two-way communication and is essential when the sands are shifting and changing quickly. Open communication helps everyone to feel they belong and are important, which in turn encourages them to be involved and to have the confidence to speak up. Effective listening, being present and tailoring 'push and pull' communication to suit differences in people and context are all part of sharing the air.

When the shadow, *stifle communication*, emerges, people dominate others or, alternatively, hoard information and foster a 'them and us' culture that blocks initiative, innovation and agility.

Share the load

Share the load is about every team member taking responsibility to play their part and collaborate with others to offer a helping hand. It is about coming together around big problems and priorities, and having each other's back by supporting each other as and when required. Giving is core to sharing the load and has many benefits including the satisfaction of succeeding as a team and knowing that others will be there for you when the going gets tough.

The shadow, *look after your own turf*, speaks for itself. People quite literally prioritise their own patch, and this often reveals itself as in-company competition, narrow self-interest and hoarding resources and information.

Share the wins and losses

Share the wins and losses reminds us that effective teams win, lose and learn together, whereas in the shadow, *play I win, you lose*, people take credit for wins while blaming losses on others.

At the heart of sharing the wins and losses is accountability for outcomes and for what can be learned from the experience. That's why celebrating successes, debriefing and capturing the learning for future improvement is core to this practice.

Applying the five shares with your team

The five shares describe the most important practices you can use to build team collaboration, as well as those that are most likely to hold you back.

Brett Wickham highlights the value of this thinking at ACCIONA Energía Australia: 'We've transformed from working very much in silos; business development developed all the projects, power marketing contracted all the power, engineering construction built them and operations operated them. Now we're looking across projects and connecting up to *share the big picture* and *share the load*.'

These elements form the basis for a primary tool, *Five shares (above the line/below the line)*.

For each of the five shares, this tool showcases behaviours or practices above and below the line (as shown in figure 12.2).

Share the big picture	Share the reality	Share the air	Share the load	Share the wins and losses
Pursue other agendas	Avoid and deny	Stifle communication	Look after your own turf	Play I win, you lose

Figure 12.2: five shares (above the line/below the line)

The tool offers:

» a shared language to describe what working as one means

» a simple and elegant way to identify team strengths and potential derailers

» a scalable framework to take across the team of teams in your organisation.

Download a pdf of the *five shares (above the line/below the line)* model from the website www.toolkitforturbulence.com.

Five shares (above the line / below the line)

Use Five Shares to build a shared understanding in your team, or wider team of teams, about what working as one team means and the potential strengths and derailers of collaboration.

INSTRUCTIONS

1. Print out or share the Five Shares model on screen and introduce the tool to your team by explaining how people and teams who collaborate within and between teams do five things differently from those who are less connected.

2. Walk through each of the five shares and their respective shadows, encouraging people to add insights on the team's current behaviours and practices and the impacts of these on team relationships, effectiveness and outcomes.

3. Guide the team to identify three strengths to continue and three behaviours or practices to start (or do more) or to stop (or do less).

4. Facilitate a conversation that draws out agreed priorities to sustain or improve your team collaboration.

Keep a copy of the model and use it as a reference.

Five Shares ... *above the line / below the line*

Above the line

Share the big picture
- [ ] We share a common purpose
- [ ] We show commitment to an agreed set of values
- [ ] Decisions are made by thinking, 'What is best for the whole?'
- [ ] We show respect by considering the impact of our actions on colleagues

Share the reality
- [ ] People feel free to speak the truth – respectfully and openly
- [ ] We give and receive useful feedback
- [ ] We deliver what we each need and expect
- [ ] We debate and make decisions based on evidence/data

Share the air
- [ ] Communication between us is open and constructive
- [ ] We follow a disciplined communication plan
- [ ] We make a concerted effort to build trust
- [ ] Our meetings and forums are productive

Share the load
- [ ] We regularly plan and prioritise together
- [ ] We treat each other as equal partners
- [ ] We collaborate successfully on problems and opportunities
- [ ] Roles and expectations are clear and aligned

Share the wins and losses
- [ ] We take accountability for results
- [ ] We debrief and capture learning so performance gets better
- [ ] We celebrate the wins and recognise progress and learning
- [ ] We succeed because of great collaboration

Below the line

Pursue other agendas
- [ ] We lack understanding of the respective situations of others
- [ ] We encourage or allow conflicting agendas to thrive between us
- [ ] Opportunities are missed because of silo thinking
- [ ] We lack alignment to the big picture

Avoid and deny
- [ ] There is a lot of 'spin' on information
- [ ] Direct, honest feedback conversations are rare
- [ ] The tough conversations/issues are usually avoided
- [ ] Reality checks are delayed or avoided

Stifle communication
- [ ] Alternative views get dismissed or criticised
- [ ] People or functions dominate the cross-business meetings
- [ ] There is too much emphasis on status and position power
- [ ] We are too guarded which inhibits trust

Look after your own turf
- [ ] We treat each other as competitors
- [ ] Planning and prioritising mostly happens in isolation
- [ ] Processes and systems cause friction and/or reduced effectiveness
- [ ] We have inconsistency in language and practices

Play I win, you lose
- [ ] People look to blame/deflect when things go wrong
- [ ] Disciplined and intensive debriefing rarely happens
- [ ] Process is more important than outcomes
- [ ] We are struggling because people feel isolated

Item A. Building trust-based relationships

In the previous chapter you learned how to build the essential foundations for team trust by gaining commitment to alignment of purpose and priorities. Reflecting on his career experience across multiple industries, Andrew McConville observes the importance of this foundation: 'Organisations crumble without alignment; trust disintegrates and individualism prevails under pressure.'

Bernadette McDonald commenced as Chief Executive of The Royal Children's Hospital Melbourne right in the middle of COVID. She was greeted with a barrage of sympathetic comments from colleagues that it must be terrible entering an organisation in crisis mode. Her mindset was completely different: 'No, it's actually really advantageous because I just got to work really quickly to build relationships and build leadership credibility,' she observes.

Every one of our advantage leaders emphasises the importance of building trust-based relationships, and they do it at three levels: with the team, across the enterprise and with stakeholders.

Trust. What do you mean?

Trust can be a slippery term to work with because it not only means different things to different people, but it also takes different forms.

In a tight-knit team trust means a high level of vulnerability, but what does that mean when you're working with other teams, strategic partners or a Board?

Striking the 'right' level of vulnerability and openness is aways a judgement call; however, these questions moved us to explore and find a better definition or model for trust.

The model we settled on is adapted from the 1990s work of Larry Reynolds described in *The Trust Effect* and captured in the acronym I-CORE (*Integrity, Competence, Openness, Reliability, Equity*) (see figure 12.3, overleaf). It has stood the test of time and has been used in many different contexts to help understand and support the building of trust.

It is described here and then introduced as a primary tool to be used in forging and strengthening partnering relationships:

» *Integrity* is the gateway to the other four items because without integrity it is difficult and potentially unwise to consider openness within a relationship where problems and vulnerabilities are exposed. Of course, it is up to you to decide how high to set the bar, perhaps remembering the beautiful words of E Lockhart when referring to the ultimate partnership: 'Love is when you give someone else the power to destroy you, and you trust them not to do it.'

» *Competence* is a prerequisite to trust in high-demand environments, because others need to be able to rely upon your ability to complete the task at hand successfully.

» *Openness* speaks to vulnerability and has two fundamental dimensions: (1) being open to others' feelings, perspectives and ideas, and (2) being transparent about yours.

» *Reliability* describes whether someone is dependable and delivers on expectations.

» *Equity* can have contested definitions; however, we recommend 'equal respect' because it is the bedrock of great team work.

I	**Integrity**	values, ethics, walking the talk
C	**Competence**	capabilities and skills
O	**Openness**	open-minded and transparent
R	**Reliability**	delivering what is expected (quality and timeliness)
E	**Equity**	treating people with equal respect

Figure 12.3: I-CORE trust model

I-CORE provides a shared and highly practical definition of trust and is a handy tool to:

» assess current and desired levels of trust among your team and partners

» identify strengths and areas of concern with relationships

» guide the plans and actions to strengthen partnering relationships.

I-CORE trust model

Use this tool as the starting point for intentionally building trust-based relationships in any context, including within your team, between colleagues and teams, and in strategic partnerships.

Competence
Demonstrating
capabilities and skills

Reliability
Delivering with quality
and timeliness

I C O R E

Integrity
Values, ethics,
walking the talk

Openness
Open mindset and
transparency

Equity
Treating others
with equal respect

INSTRUCTIONS

1. Familiarise yourself with the meaning of each of the five I-CORE elements in the model and why it is important to building trust-based relationships.

2. Use I-CORE to evaluate important relationships within your team, with colleagues and with stakeholders. Try using a five-point rating scale (1 = Not at all to 5 = Absolutely) for each of the five I-CORE elements. We recommend that you start with your team, as this will allow you to become familiar with the tool and the way people react to it.

3. Deploy the techniques and practices we outline throughout this chapter to improve trust-based relationships in your team and beyond. Just choose the most important areas of concern and avoid the temptation to tackle too many at the same time.

4. Regularly reflect on I-CORE for any important team or individual relationship and remember, building trust is a two-way street. This means it may be helpful, if a bit confronting, to check how others view you and your team on the I-CORE rating scale.

Keep a copy of this model and use it as a reference for yourself and your team.

Trust in relationships

Creating and sustaining team trust can be challenging, particularly in leadership teams where there are natural tensions between the leaders of different functions. Organisations need some push and pull between leaders so diverse perspectives are debated and effective decisions made. So here sits yet another paradox: *how to build trust while encouraging the contest of ideas?*

The elements of I-CORE provide immediate insights, because trust requires people to know one another's character, capabilities and style. That starts with building relationships, and to do that you must create opportunities for people to get to know each other as people. Saying that building relationships is important is one thing; doing it in a busy, dispersed environment is another. It takes a deliberate investment in time and energy to make it happen.

As a leader, you must be willing to commit time and effort to building relationships, irrespective of the reluctance of others to spend time on activities that don't 'shift the dial' on their perceived current priorities.

Teams that fail to prioritise building relationships run the risk that members get to know each other only 'in role' and know little about each other outside of that identity. When the pressure cooker heats up and they don't have a strong I-CORE frame, it's highly likely they underachieve due to conflict, fragmentation, avoidance or poor decision making.

Traditionally, relationship building has been sidelined to an offsite meeting with the customary team-building exercises. These activities usually focus on the team as a whole, and that's important; however, we believe it is also essential for people to build interpersonal connections by sharing stories and coaching each other in smaller groups. Our experience is that people will be more vulnerable and open to receiving insights, feedback and support in smaller groups before opening themselves up to the group as a whole.

Here are two ideas with associated tools you can use during offsite team-building sessions or as a supplement to team meetings on a regular basis.

1.	**2.**
Personal stories	*Colleague coaching*
Sharing personal stories about important events that shaped character and approaches to teamwork and leadership	Working in pairs and threes to actively coach and support each other's performance and wellbeing

1. Personal stories

Strengthening relationships and trust is particularly important when forming your team, integrating new members or starting a new phase. That's where personal stories can be valuable and the structure and agenda matter less than four essential aspects of the activity itself:

» *Informal context.* Find a setting that encourages people to step out of their usual roles and be open and reflective such as an offsite venue or a coffee session in a more relaxed environment.

» *Leader led.* Go first because your example will set the tone for courage and vulnerability and send the message that this is a safe place to share personal stories and experiences.

» *Confidentiality and care.* Expect a few tears or surprises. Confidentiality is essential, as is showing care and respect for colleagues who take risks and share intensely personal stories.

» *Optional participation.* To ensure safety be sure to give people the choice to opt in or opt out at any stage, and also be alert in case the personal sharing raises issues for people that need further care.

Personal stories

Personal stories is a particularly effective way to build team relationships because it combines vulnerability with greater awareness of each other's background and drivers.

INSTRUCTIONS

1. **Set the tone.** Gauge your team's needs and adjust accordingly. For instance, when introducing personal stories with VCE, we started in pairs to establish confidence and trust before sharing with the whole group.

2. **Prepare for sharing.** Choose a suitable time and place and brief your team on what to expect. Encourage them to identify up to three life experiences that have significantly shaped them and their lives. Make a deliberate decision at this point whether to split people into smaller groups of two or three to share their life experiences or to share with the group as a whole.

3. **Respect differences.** Be mindful and accepting of privacy and psychological safety. Encourage and allow people to share at their own comfort level, with 10–15 minutes per team member and time for reflection, exploration and debriefing.

4. **Lead by example.** Begin the sharing yourself and encourage others to follow in a suitable order. Thank each person for their contribution and take breaks as needed. End by reiterating confidentiality and providing any required support.

Note: This activity is particularly valuable for leadership teams to build trust-based relationships and navigate power dynamics.

2. Colleague coaching

'Colleague coaching' is the practice of team members actively engaging in coaching one another by providing valuable insights, constructive feedback, and challenging perspectives to address workplace issues and navigate professional challenges together.

A regular practice of colleague coaching can open up deeper dialogue between team members, encourage care and support, and boost awareness and capability by sharing understanding and best practice. Use *colleague coaching* to supplement your team development, planning and problem solving by using the secondary tool, Colleague Coaching.

Recap

Building trust-based relationships is one of your most important leadership tasks, so activities like personal storytelling and colleague coaching are extremely useful. The time invested will help drive mutual respect, understanding and support. These conversations will also lay the groundwork for open communication, less conflict, and more opportunities for collaboration and growth.

Colleague coaching

Colleague coaching can be used to supplement your team development, planning and problem solving.

INSTRUCTIONS

1. Introduce colleague coaching by explaining that you see value in creating a team culture of supporting and challenging each other by sharing insights, feedback and best practices.

2. Split the group into pairs (preferably) or threes if that's not possible. Explain that there are three ground rules for the activity:

   a. **One coachee at a time.** In any conversation one person plays the role of coachee, so it is 'their world' that is the focus of the conversation. The other person or people are the coach.

   b. **Insights, not small talk.** The aim of the coach is to draw out 'insights' that have a positive impact on the coachee and the team as a whole. That may include reflection from past events, processing feedback, or developing new perspectives and ideas. Be very mindful that the focus remain on the world of the coachee.

   c. **Confidentiality is a must.** The conversation is confidential unless all members agree that it can be shared outside the group.

3. Provide a framework and timeframe for the conversation. The conversation can be framed by a question, such as, 'What's the most challenging question you need to answer in this next period?' A guide to timeline: 20–30 minutes.

4. Facilitate a team debrief to discuss the process rather than the outcome. Draw out what people find most valuable from the conversations by asking the question, 'What would you like your colleague coaches to do more of in future sessions to have an even greater positive impact?'

Item B. Make partnerships as important as teams

Most organisations allocate funding for team building; however, ask an executive if they have a budget for partnership building and chances are you will receive uncertain or even evasive answers:

» 'Our engagement team handles that.'

» 'We do it as part of team building.'

» 'Yes, we're very deliberate about the way we build our strategic partnerships.'

» 'Hmm, never given that any thought.'

Ten years ago, the primary operating structure was unquestionably the team; however, technology, customer-centric thinking and sheer pace can and must transform conventional team structures into a vibrant network of connections between people.

Teams remain essential to aggregate capability, make effective decisions and provide a sense of belonging; however, the reality is most things don't get done between teams, they get done between people. People are based in teams, but it's their own ability to connect and partner with others inside or outside the organisation that unlocks (or blocks) potential.

Chris Tanti has observed the strong and rapid shift towards partnership thinking at the Leukaemia Foundation: 'When one of us is having conversations with government, then it's going to affect our communications, our fundraising and other operations, so that leader must anticipate the impacts on the rest of the organisation. We've put the spotlight on accelerating this style of partnering between leaders and teams because that's not been the traditional way of doing things.'

Linear challenges can often be met without effective relationships; however, the opposite is true for nonlinear challenges where connection and partnering are essential.

Across the boundaries

When building your own team and strategic relationships with others, it's wise to be aware that functions, hierarchy and location can and do create barriers to collaboration, as do local work cultures and differences in values and personalities. You need to develop a way to engage colleagues, teams and stakeholders across conventional boundaries and differences.

One of Robert Iervasi's first learnings from COVID-19 was how the infrastructure of a building can be a barrier to people collaborating with others who have the same goal or objective in mind. 'When you have a building, you've got walls and offices, and even if it's open plan, it tends to reinforce hierarchy because it's visible, and even creates a discipline to respect and acknowledge hierarchy. When COVID-19 hit it was all Teams or Zoom and there was a need for organisations to shift to bring people together who are relevant to the project or initiative. Hierarchy disappears, becoming almost irrelevant and invisible. It doesn't matter who reported to whom.'

Crisis often opens up possibilities for partnering and collaboration across the conventional boundaries, but things will settle back into their old ways unless, as Robert Iervasi half-jokingly suggests, you 'put that in a bottle and roll it out across the whole organisation'.

A mindset for partnering

One of the critical requirements of leading and navigating in nonlinear environments is the ability to establish and sustain partnering relationships. The reasons are clear: partners are better at aligning their values and goals, better at resolving challenging problems, and more likely to learn and adapt when things get tough.

Partnering in business is both a mindset and a relationship. The starting mindset is commitment to a shared big picture, which may be a goal, a vision or values. The relationship is built on trust and sustained by being open and caring, tackling problems together and taking the longer-term view. A strong partnering relationship exemplifies the Five Shares: share the big picture, share the reality, share the air, share the load, and share the wins and losses.

A word of caution: it is fanciful to think that it is desirable or even possible for every person or team in an enterprise to work in a strong partnering relationship with every other. However, it is both possible and desirable to:

> » be clear on the most important partnering relationships for you and your team

> » have practical partnering tools to align and deliver on expectations

> » commit to act as a partner when significant enterprise problems or opportunities arise.

This means you need to be clear who to partner with and how to partner effectively.

For any relationship where strengthening the partnering is important, our recommended primary tool is the *Partnering Quadrant in action*. This can be used informally as a framework to guide your thinking and actions, or as a template to establish a formal partnering agreement.

Introducing the Partnering Quadrant

The Partnering Quadrant is a model that describes the four essential steps to building and sustaining trust-based partnering relationships. Think about each quadrant as a conversation between colleagues, between teams or with a stakeholder.

Each of the four conversations (see figure 12.4) has a specific and important intent, which is explained here and then integrated into the primary tool *Partnering Quadrant in action* and the accompanying Partnering Quadrant Canvas.

Q1 Create rapport and empathy	**Q2** Understand expectations
Q3 Establish agreements	**Q4** Grow the partnership (ACL)

Figure 12.4: Partnering Quadrant model

Quadrant 1. Create rapport and empathy

It is common that people and teams enter relationships in a 'task-focused' way, failing to take the time to understand the other's needs, including their hopes and concerns and the context in which they are operating. As friction arises the relationship is at risk because people inevitably misunderstand the 'why' behind actions or inactions.

The conversation in quadrant 1 will reduce those risks by creating rapport, understanding and empathy, laying the foundation for a genuine partnering relationship. The Partnering Quadrant Canvas highlights three key items that are important to share in the conversation: *vision, goals and aspirations, values and principles,* and *pain points and pressures.*

Quadrant 2. Understand expectations

Partnering is about trust…and trust is about meeting each other's expectations.

The I-CORE model is important to keep in mind here, as expectations need to be aligned for *integrity, competence, openness, reliability* and *equity*.

The conversation in quadrant 2 will help to draw out the implicit expectations about task (outputs and outcomes) and people (communication and behaviours) and make these explicit. For example, there may be expectations about quality, speed or style of communication that are assumed but not aligned, and it is here that potentially disastrous misunderstandings and disconnects can be avoided. The canvas highlights three topics for conversation: *outcomes and timeframes, outputs and milestones,* and *behaviours and style.*

Quadrant 3. Establish agreements

In a strong partnership the expectations of one party are matched by the commitments (and actions) of the other, which in turn builds trust and confidence in all the I-CORE aspects. Accordingly, the next step after openly sharing expectations is to define realistic agreements.

The conversation in quadrant 3 enables the framing of explicit two-way agreements including outcomes, timeframes and behaviours. In the early stages of partnering those agreements might cover only a small number of items to 'test and learn', while later this can become a core framework for cross-organisational teamwork. The canvas prompts conversations in three areas: *common ground, realistic agreements,* and *commitment to task and people.* The latter is intended to draw out commitment to getting things done and to doing it in a way that reflects commitment to partnering.

Quadrant 4. Grow the partnership

An effective partnering relationship will be a living example of the ACL loop, so the conversations in the final quadrant address questions about the tempo of communication and learning.

Quadrant 4 conversations ensure the alignment, collaboration and learning by defining the frequency of updates and check-ins, calling out potential friction points in advance and ensuring the relationship is set up for success by building a debriefing routine. The canvas prompts are: *regular communication*, *anticipated friction points*, and *discipline of the debrief*.

An observation

When people and teams come together with the intent to work as partners, the most common mistake is to ignore quadrant 1 and go straight to quadrant 2. They start sharing expectations, then they settle on an agreement and all but ignore quadrant 4. When turbulence hits they're back into conflict, instead of having the advantage of a strong ACL connection built on shared understanding and respect for each other's circumstances. To avoid those risks, follow the instructions overleaf to complete the primary tool *Partnering Quadrant in action* and the accompanying Partnering Quadrant Canvas

Implementing the Partnering Quadrant

Use the Partnering Quadrant to guide all types of formal and informal partnering relationships including between teams, with colleagues and with stakeholders. If using informally, keep in mind the intent of each quadrant and adjust the agenda of your conversations accordingly. If used formally, the Partnering Quadrant Canvas provides an excellent framework to guide conversations and to create an alternative to the more limiting service-level agreement approach.

We have used this format to guide the building of countless one-to-one relationships right through to facilitating detailed agreements between international teams, one of which required strong partnering covering nine global sites and 11000 people.

The instructions for the primary tool are targeted at team-to-team partnering. Visit the website www.toolkitforturbulence.com to download further support resources.

Partnering Quadrant in action

Use this tool to guide your efforts to build formal and informal partnering relationships between teams, colleagues and stakeholders. This version of the tool is designed for team-to-team partnering.

INSTRUCTIONS

1. Select another team with whom you want to strengthen collaboration.

2. Use I-CORE to assess the current relationship between the teams.

3. Contact the other team leader and explain your wish to apply the Partnering Quadrant as a tool to guide team-to-team conversations.

4. If they agree, commit both teams to prepare for a joint session by considering quadrants 1 and 2 in detail, and any important items in 3 and 4.

5. Consider a neutral facilitator if conflict is likely and be mindful this may require two meetings to fully cover and lock down agreements.

6. Start with a brief Partnering Quadrant Canvas overview emphasising why each of the four aspects are important. Record insights and set ground rules such as:

   » Share hopes and concerns openly

   » Show curiosity, ask, listen

   » Find common ground

   » Reach clear agreements

   » Commit to communication rhythm.

7. Close off by agreeing the form of the write up and the immediate actions.

Partnering Quadrant Canvas

1 Create rapport and empathy

- Vision, goals and aspirations
- Values and principles
- Pain points and pressures

2 Understand expectations

- Outcomes and timeframes
- Outputs and milestones
- Behaviours and style

3 Establish agreements

- Common ground
- Realistic agreements
- Commitment to task and people

4 Grow the partnership

- Regular communication
- Anticipated friction points
- Discipline of the debrief

Recap

Collaboration is a must for teams to seize opportunities and avoid the pitfalls of being disconnected and working at cross-purposes. To truly collaborate, teams require strong connections and synergies inside and outside of the team. This means building healthy interpersonal trust and forging strong partnerships; anything less is simply not good enough.

We will now take you one step further as we look at how to master collaborative problem solving and team-based decision making to achieve synergy.

BUILDING BLOCK

 # Synergy

The pathway from disruption to advantage is littered with challenges. Irrespective of the nature of the turbulence, however, advantage leaders use their biggest problems as a force multiplier to fuel a culture of collaboration and innovation.

In Defence Science and Technology Group, Professor Tanya Monro and her team deploy cross-functional teams to develop new defence capabilities at pace and scale by problem solving and co-creating with stakeholders from industry and universities.

In a manufacturing setting, Robert Iervasi tackles supply-chain disruption head on by leveraging small, fast cross-functional teams to develop innovative cross-business solutions.

Bringing together cross-functional teams to solve complex problems not only helps breakthroughs and addresses immediate challenges but also fosters collaboration and enhances collective capabilities.

Item A. Problem solving and co-creation

One of the keys to creating a collaborative environment is to provide people with shared tools such as design thinking, lean or agile methodologies, to help cross-functional teams and experts to work together effectively. These tools provide a structured approach to problem solving and encourage creative thinking, rapid prototyping and iteration.

One tool has proven itself time and again to give everyone in a cross-functional team a shared language and process to follow. That tool is the PROBED problem solver, which we have deployed everywhere from the Prime Minister's Office to frontline teams in developing countries as part of the Think One Team method.

PROBED addresses six key elements (**P**roblem. **R**ealities, **O**ptions, **B**est option, **E**xecution, **D**o next) and can be used within wider methodologies (such as lean and agile) to bring cross-functional teams together to address bottlenecks and barriers, create new solutions, improve existing products and services, and drive growth and innovation.

PROBED collaborative problem solver

Collaborative problem solving means surfacing and tackling problems together to deliver better outcomes. It is about co-creating breakthrough solutions to important problems by working in small teams across traditional boundaries (functions, specialties, hierarchies, business units).

Having a shared tool-based approach to collaborative problem solving helps to tap the collective intelligence of the team or the whole enterprise.

The capabilities and practices of collaborative problem solving are among the most important contributors to team agility, and a tool like PROBED brings many immediate and longer-term benefits:

> » *Clarity*. People clearly understand the real problems and their root causes.

> » *Ownership and impact*. Unclaimed problems are owned and 'wrestled to the ground'.

> » *Pace*. Small, fast teams reduce the time required to resolve problems.

» *Elephants.* The 'elephants in the room' are brought into the open and addressed constructively.

» *Capability.* Diverse people and teams learn a shared language and approach to problem solving.

You can use PROBED as the starting point for any type of problem and in any setting—as a personal tool to help you think through an issue, with a team to guide the conversations, online as a template in a crowdsourcing approach or in a host of other ways.

The simple yet powerful PROBED framework uses the three natural steps in any problem-solving process (*analyse – create – execute*) to provide a method and language for problem solving that anyone can use.

The strengths of PROBED lie in the simplicity of the six core questions:

P	*What is the **P**roblem?*
R	*What are the **R**ealities (causes, effects etc.)?*
O	*What are the **O**ptions?*
B	*What is the **B**est option?*
E	*What is the **E**xecution plan?*
D	*What do we **D**o next?*

These questions frame the steps outlined in the PROBED Canvas. The six PROBED items provide a clear and consistent template for problem-solving conversations and presenting the outputs. This equips team members and partners to speak the same language, which can make meetings more efficient and allow problems to be solved faster

And remember, the PROBED tool is a gem because it integrates with any other methodology.

PROBED collaborative problem solver

Use PROBED as a personal and team problem solving and communication tool.

INSTRUCTIONS

1. **Choose a problem.** Select a suitable problem to facilitate the PROBED approach.

2. **Prepare the group.** Introduce the PROBED Canvas and walk through the six elements. Explain how it does not have to be a linear process, and that you can add other tools along the way. (Some people who are trained in more comprehensive processes sometimes think PROBED is too simple. Reassure them that PROBED can be easily folded into more sophisticated methodologies but is a very useful first step.)

3. **Use a visual.** Use a whiteboard, flipchart or online tool to capture the conversation so people see the content as it unfolds.

4. **Facilitate the framework.** Follow the PROBED facilitation steps for a range of prompting questions to guide the process. Remember to play the facilitator/coach role rather than positioning yourself as the expert or boss because this will help to empower your team and also build their problem-solving capability.

5. **Close off.** Finish with a debrief and clear set of actions including confirming who will document and publish the outputs.

PROBED Canvas   *Collaborative problem solving tool*

P **Problem**
What is the problem?

O **Options**
What are the options?

E **Execute**
What is the execution plan?

R **Realities**
What are the realities?

B **Best options**
What is the best option?

D **Do next**
What do we do next?

PROBED facilitation steps

When using the PROBED Canvas here are prompting questions and associated facilitation tips for each of the six steps.

P Problem

Many teams wander into conversations about problems without a clear sense of what they are trying to solve, or how to do that in an effective and efficient way. Start by getting a basic statement or set of bullet points to scope the issue you want to address. Prompting questions include:

» What's the core problem to address?

» Can we write it as a statement or set of bullet points?

» Is this one problem or can we break it up?

Tip: Avoid perfection, rapidly develop a draft problem statement and move on to Realities.

R Realities

This is the most important step in the process and where to spend the most time. Get to this as soon as you have a basic statement of the problem, so the team focuses on understanding the underlying context and causes. Prompting questions include:

» What seem to be the key causes of this problem?

» What context is important and might be contributing to the problem?

» What strengths or weaknesses in the ways of working need considering?

Treat this like brainstorming and produce as many items as possible. Then sort the list into categories. For example, if the problem is about communication the categories might include types of communication, systems, culture, skills and capabilities, and so on.

Tip: Look through the categories to identify potential root causes of the problem, then go back to the first item on the canvas and guide the team to rewrite the problem statement into a goal.

O Options

You have identified potential causes of the problem; now bring creativity to find options to resolve those causes. For example, if one of the potential causes of poor communication is lack of skills and capabilities then explore different ways to address that issue. Prompting questions include:

» What are the obvious options here to address the key causes of the problem?

» How can we think about this from a different angle?

» What assumptions need challenging?

Tip: Make sure everyone is heard and diverse perspectives are supported and captured.

B Best option

You have developed a range of options to resolve the problem, so now it's time to sort or combine those to choose the best way forward. Here are some prompting questions:

» What tests or criteria do the best options need to meet?

» Can we combine options to make them stronger?

» Is there more work to be done to find breakthrough ideas?

Tip: Be clear on your criteria to make the decision about the best option(s) and be open to further exploring if you feel that the options lack the potential to break through and get a good outcome.

E Execution

When you have chosen the best option(s) it is essential to get clarity and commitment to the actions. Here are the prompting questions:

» What are the 'three Ws' for each of our options — What, Who, When?

» What resources and support will be needed to execute this successfully?

» Are the outcomes clear? For example, do we know what 'done' means?

Tip: Make sure the desired outcomes and actions are clear and agreed, including accountabilities.

D Do next

This final step is just an extension of Execution, but it's included because you will want to create action, not just agreement to action. That's why the prompting questions are all about making things happen:

» What are the first steps and when will they happen?

» Are we committed to making it happen?

» Who will write up the PROBED notes from this activity?

Tip: Confirm the accountabilities and timelines so you are confident that action will happen.

Recap

Shared methodologies and tools like PROBED help to promote a strong team culture where members collaborate and work together seamlessly. The tools reduce the time it takes to tackle issues, resulting in faster delivery and an increased capacity to take on more projects and initiatives.

Item B. Decision making

When Russia invaded Ukraine in February 2022 the US did what most of the world expected: it offered to evacuate President Volodymyr Zelensky from the capital Kyiv to a safe haven. What happened next was not expected.

Instead of seizing the opportunity to escape to safety, his response was both brave and belligerent. The Ukraine embassy proudly conveyed to the world their President's decision: 'The fight is here. I don't need a ride, I need ammunition.'

Imagine being in that position. Having to make that decision. We can all just wonder what we might do. Could we think rationally enough to make the right call?

Human decision making is a tricky business at the best of times, and few know better than Princeton University psychologist and economist Daniel Kahneman, who won a Nobel Prize, alongside colleague Amos Tversky, for his Prospect Theory, in which he proposed that rather than being the rational decision makers we claim to be, humans are chronic shortcut takers, and this can actually cause us to make poor judgement calls about risk.

When your team gets together to make a decision they bring with them all the challenges Kahneman identified, along with anything up to 200 cognitive biases that can affect rational decision making, and that's before considering the implications of two thinking systems — one fast, instinctive and based on emotion, and the other slower and more deliberative — described in Kahneman's best-selling book *Thinking, Fast and Slow*. And, you'd be right in guessing that the two don't always synchronise well!

So how do teams minimise the risks of biases and shortcuts when making crucial decisions in a context where fear and anxiety are prevalent? That's our next step on this journey.

Three showstoppers

Conventional wisdom has it that the big decisions are made behind closed doors by the Executive but that's not what's happening among advantage leaders.

Teams are being empowered to co-create most big decisions, so they collectively own not only the decision but its successful implementation.

Robert Iervasi describes his approach: 'Ensure you are focusing on longer term growth, longer term ambitions, engagement and getting everyone on board. So, adopt a collaborative style where you remain driven to achieve the right outcomes and goals, but making sure you've got the inputs of all the diverse thinkers around the table to get there.'

Taking on two roles, the leader:

> » curates the environment and conversations (sometimes supported by an independent facilitator)

> » closes out decisions when required.

As the leader and/or member of a team facing tough calls in turbulent conditions, there are at least three things you don't want:

1. *Impasse.* The team fails to break through groupthink or paralysis and misses the opportunity.

2. *Implosion.* The team does break through but implodes because of conflict and damage arising from the experience or outcome.

3. *Retreat.* The team makes a good decision in a constructive way but then retreats after the meeting.

Take a few moments to reflect on the extent to which these are risks for your team.

INSIGHT EXERCISE
Reflection on the decision risks

Reflect on potential 'showstopper' risks in your team when making important decisions. The rating scale is 1 = Not at all to 5 = All the time.

Team risk indicators	1	2	3	4	5
1. People stay silent and/or agree for the sake of harmony.	o	o	o	o	o
2. There is unspoken conflict never raised in the full group.	o	o	o	o	o
3. People rarely challenge you and/or their colleagues.	o	o	o	o	o
4. Important perspectives are not represented.	o	o	o	o	o
5. The team procrastinate by seeking more data or time.	o	o	o	o	o
6. People shy away from stating their position on a decision.	o	o	o	o	o
7. Some members may feel excluded from the decision.	o	o	o	o	o
8. Some members may feel railroaded by the robust debate.	o	o	o	o	o

Items 1–4 are primarily about the risk of groupthink, while items 5–6 are about paralysis by analysis and 7–8 are about leaving people behind.

Do you see any areas of concern for your team as you set up for the challenging decisions that lie ahead?

Reduce the decision risks

Close the gate is a handy tool when facing particularly controversial or difficult conversations where there is the risk of impasses and implosions. It includes the following three steps:

Step 1	Step 2	Step 3
Frame the conversations.	*Use decision principles.*	*Close the gate.*

These steps are designed to help avoid an impasse, implosion or retreat when making an important decision where you want 100 per cent team commitment.

The tool, *Close the Gate* (overleaf), gives you four questions that must be answered in Step 3, together with a Facilitation Guide to navigate the process.

Close the gate

Close the Gate is a set of four questions and a process to follow when you know your team is facing a challenging decision.

INSTRUCTIONS

1. **Read the facilitation guide.** The guide takes you through the three steps to frame the conversation, agree decision principles and close the gate.

2. **Review the Decision Principles.** The Decision Principles provide an example which will help you to guide your team to select their principles. Review these before the session begins.

3. **Familiarise with the Gates.** The tool features four questions, and each is treated like a gate. In other words, you facilitate the team conversation but don't move to the next gate until there is 100 per cent agreement. Here are the four questions which are self explanatory:

   Gate 1. Is what we are deciding clear? If the answer is yes, then move on.

   Gate 2. Is it aligned to our principles? Once debated, adjusted and agreed, then move on.

   Gate 3. Are there any showstoppers? If none are identified, then move on. If some are, test and validate. If they really are showstoppers then pause the process and return to the problem.

   Gate 4. Is this a team decision or a leader call? If it's a team decision, then ask everyone to commit to the decision — in other words, close the gate behind the decision. If it's decided that it's your call, then make the decision and remind your team that the gate is closed behind the decision.

4. **Facilitate through to outcome.** This process can be time consuming and difficult when a team becomes blocked. Be prepared to use your other tools (e.g. PROBED) to dig into what's creating the unwillingness in your team to move on. If all else fails and the decision has to be made, go to gate 4.

Facilitation guide

Step 1. Frame the conversation for quality debate

When a meeting is convened and difficult decisions are anticipated, be deliberate in setting up the vital aspects: a clear intent so people know what success means for the meeting, the right tone so that the dialogue is constructive and a focused agenda to avoid distraction. Revisit your team purpose and team commitments early in the meeting to reinforce the responsibility of each person to contribute to making it constructive and successful. Position this exercise as an opportunity to test and strengthen team unity, but be clear that today it's about making a decision.

Step 2. Review and agree on your decision principles

We have found value in working with teams prior to the 'heavy lifting' sessions, or at the outset if needed, to develop an agreed set of decision-making principles. These can be invaluable in providing structure to the decision process.

Following is an example of decision-making principles from a very effective leadership team.

- » *Be true to our core.* Prioritise what is central to the purpose of the organisation.
- » *Stay true to our values and culture.* Treat everyone with respect.
- » *Be bold.* This can't be about incrementalism.
- » *Rely on evidence.* Use evidence and analysis to judge impact.
- » *Be clever.* Connect and integrate people, technology, systems and resources.
- » *Play a long game.* Aim for sustainable benefits.

Step 3. Close the gate

Facilitate the team conversation through each gate, being sure to gain 100 per cent agreement before moving to the next gate. As highlighted in the Instructions, this can be painstaking but 'hold your shape' and guide the team to lock in behind the decision.

Recap

In turbulence the immediacy and frequency of decision making increase, along with the risks of impasses and implosions when the stakes are high. Sally Capp closes this chapter with an excellent reminder for leadership teams: 'The ability to make decisions is what sets leaders apart. You need to have a strong resolve to do that in pressure situations.'

Learnings

» To collaborate is to **share** in a spirit of working as one, because without sharing there is inevitably waste, missed opportunities, disengagement, and the risks that come from silos and poorly executed strategies. Working as one requires connection and synergy.

» Healthy interpersonal **trust** among team members and **partnering** relationships are the foundations of strong connection in your team and with others.

» A focus on synergy will improve team **collaboration** and **decision making.**

» Think **I-CORE** when seeking to build and sustain trust-based relationships.

» The **Partnering Quadrant** is an excellent framework to guide the development of partnering relationships between colleagues and teams and with stakeholders.

» **PROBED** is a simple and effective tool to engage and empower everyone as problems solvers.

» Decision making needs to be curated in a way that enables you to **close the gate** behind the decision with the confidence that all will support it.

CHAPTER 13

Make team learning a habit

How do you create a team culture of reflection, openness and two-way feedback? How can dynamic learning be embedded into everyday action? What's the optimal tempo to sustain team adaptability and performance?

Open, agile and adaptable teams have an advantage in disrupted environments because they have mastered the ability to learn at pace and on the run.

To build this team capability for fast learning requires awareness, which comes from openness to feedback and relentless debriefing. In addition, to sustain pace and to deliver without being too reactive requires a disciplined tempo or operating rhythm. This provides the predictable 'drumbeat' for learning and realigning when conditions change, and will help you drive empowerment and accountability.

This chapter focuses on Dynamic Team Learning and two building blocks defined on the Team Canvas, *awareness* and *tempo*.

Learn

5 **Awareness**

A Openness to reflect, give and receive feedback and to challenge

B Relentless debriefing

6 **Tempo**

A Disciplined operating rhythm/performance cycle cadence

B Delivering outcomes at pace through empowerment and accountability

BUILDING BLOCK
----

⑤ Awareness

Self and team awareness form the bedrock for learning and adapting effectively in high-demand, volatile conditions because without awareness, individuals and teams are at risk of drifting, susceptible to unseen vulnerabilities and unable to navigate the ever-changing landscape with precision and agility.

Team culture

Openness is one of the most enduring characteristics of high-performing teams. It comes from habits such as two-way feedback, challenging conversations, reflection and debriefing, which require the team culture of trust that we discussed in the previous chapter.

These habits can be strengths, but their absence also makes them potential derailers. That means they are important to consider as you construct your toolkit for turbulence. Here's why:

> » **Reflection** is essential for personal growth and for team learning; however, failing to make it a priority risks creating blind spots that can become showstoppers in fast-changing conditions.

> » **Feedback** is equally important for individual team members and the team as a whole because it provides valuable insights into strengths and areas for improvement.

> » **Challenging** each other's ideas and assumptions is the foundation for strong and robust dialogue, which contributes to good-quality decisions. Constructive challenging helps to draw out different perspectives, interrogate issues and connect the dots between them.

> » **Debriefing** is a must-do for any team operating in turbulence because it enables fast adaptation based on what's happening and what's being learned.

Let's start by exploring the first three practices then do a deeper dive into what we call *relentless debriefing*.

Item A. Openness — reflect, feedback and challenge

If you visit The Royal Children's Hospital Melbourne on a Wednesday morning you might bump into Bernadette McDonald or another of her Executive Team on what they call an 'Exec Wednesday wander'.

For the first half hour of executive meetings everyone peels off to visit an area of the hospital. Bernadette explains: 'They pop in, say "Hi, how are things going? Anything you need?" That sort of thing. So the executive is much more visible now, including me. And people love it. They really love it.'

This style of openness by leaders is one of the biggest changes we've observed in recent years, and it brings all manner of benefits on top of visibility and connection.

From hospitals to energy companies, banks to universities, openness and informality are common themes in how advantage leaders build relationships and keep people connected in a fast-changing, hybrid world.

Brett Wickham confirms: 'We've changed the way we connect and continue to push this informal frequent getting together because, being global and growing so fast, one of our biggest risks from turbulence is people being disconnected, which can affect their wellbeing and overall performance.'

Advantage leaders prioritise being open to people throughout their organisation, but this can be hindered by siloed thinking, fear of conflict and a preference for harmony over sharing constructive feedback. Overcoming these barriers is essential to create and lead an effective team. Here are three proven practices:

Practice 1.	Practice 2.	Practice 3.
Self and team reflection	*Two-way feedback*	*Constructive challenging*

Practice 1. Self and team reflection

Self-reflection is the process of looking inward to explore your own thoughts, feelings and actions. It might be as simple as wondering what you'd prefer to do next weekend, or as deep as seeking to discover your life purpose.

In the search for learning and growth, few things are more important than self-reflection. Without it we may miss opportunities to adapt and we are at risk of being misled by blind spots such as misunderstanding our strengths and weaknesses or underestimating the impact we have on others.

INSIGHT EXERCISE
Self-reflection

Self-reflection is best understood by doing it, so here's an activity that describes three types of self-reflection. Try it when you have a spare 15–20 minutes and jot down your thoughts in a notebook or journal (because that's a great way to get the most impact from self-reflection). Encourage your team to do the same.

Reflection on an experience

Choose a recent work event that was emotionally charged:

» What happened?

» How did you feel and what generated those feelings?

» Is there an insight or learning you can take from the experience?

Reflection on thinking

Choose a complex issue you have been grappling with recently:

» What assumptions and beliefs have you brought to this issue?

» How have those assumptions and beliefs shaped your approach?

» What alternative approaches have you not yet explored?

Reflection on a surprising event

» What surprised you?

» What does this reveal about you?

» What can you take away from this experience?

The power of the pause

One of the biggest impediments to effective reflection is busyness and the associated absence of time devoted to genuine reflection.

That's why a practice like *colleague coaching* is so valuable, because it creates dedicated time for reflection and has the added benefit of a 'second mind' to help draw out new perspectives.

One of the most important things you can do as a leader is to pause and encourage personal and team reflection. You'll learn a process called *performance partnering* in the next section, but at a minimum this means scheduling dedicated time for one-on-one check-ins with team members. These are opportunities to ask, 'What achievement are you most proud of from the past week?' or, 'Which partnering relationships need the most attention?' to prompt reflection and facilitate learning and development.

Care Connect uses an approach they call 'Connect-in' to drive effective 1x1 conversations. Paul Ostrowski observes, 'It is as simple as a one-to-one meeting to check in on how people are doing; however, it's the discipline we put around Connect-ins that is the key. It has a very clear purpose and uses metrics to ensure alignment and adaptability when we're off track.'

Most of the tools we cover in this chapter are designed for enhancing self and team reflection. They all require you as leader to prioritise and model pausing and reflection.

Practice 2. Two-way feedback/insights

Most of us are not naturally wired to start the day thinking, *I hope I get some constructive feedback from someone today*, yet high-quality, honest and regular feedback is one of the most important contributors to development and performance.

Feedback comes in many forms, valid or invalid, clear or confused, so it's important to have a suitable filter to guide the way you respond. The secondary tool *3 Rs of feedback* is a handy tool for that purpose and also serves as a reminder to reflect on whether feedback is triggering your threat response.

3 Rs of feedback

When receiving challenging feedback there is always a risk of reacting negatively to the person providing the feedback or not dealing with it effectively.

The simple *3 Rs* model below highlights three phases or steps to take, irrespective of the source or nature of the feedback, to effectively receive, reflect and respond.

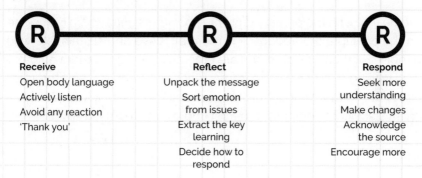

Receive	Reflect	Respond
Open body language	Unpack the message	Seek more understanding
Actively listen	Sort emotion from issues	Make changes
Avoid any reaction	Extract the key learning	Acknowledge the source
'Thank you'	Decide how to respond	Encourage more

INSTRUCTIONS

Next time you receive slightly challenging feedback see whether you can genuinely pace yourself to receive, reflect, and then respond:

1. **Receive.** Be open to receive the feedback.

2. **Reflect.** Take your time to unpack the messages.

3. **Respond.** Act on what is most valuable, and be open to further feedback.

Keep this tool handy to coach your team and colleagues to foster a feedback culture.

SEEK INSIGHTS FIRST

High-performing teams have a simple feedback principle: *Seek it first before giving it to others*.

There are several reasons why seeking feedback is preferable to the more traditional method of waiting to receive it from others. People find it less threatening from both perspectives (giver and receiver), it fosters a culture of openness, and when woven into the team operating rhythm seeking insights is a great way to accelerate learning and development.

We do that with the primary tool *Three points insights*, which is designed on the principle that feedback is more effective and sustainable when people call them 'insights' and are proactive in seeking them out rather than waiting to receive more formal feedback. People report this is less stressful and more impactful than conventional feedback conversations and a significant contributor to trust and overall team learning.

Three points insights

The *Three points insights* tool guides team members to practise and reinforce the value of regular conversations where they seek insights and feedback from colleagues.

INSTRUCTIONS

1. In advance of introducing the tool to the whole team, pre-brief two colleagues that you will be using the *Three points insights* tool. Explain its purpose and ask if they are willing to offer you insights in the team meeting as a demonstration of the approach.

2. If your colleagues agree, tell them that you will be asking the following question:

   'What specific things can I do differently to improve my positive impact on the performance and wellbeing of the team?'

3. Introduce the tool to the full team and walk through the four steps using yourself as the example:

   Step 1. Choose the question to frame the insights you want. For example, the style of question can be specific, such as your choice for the demonstration, or more general, such as 'How can I be a better team colleague to you?'

   Step 2. Explain that you have already asked two colleagues to offer insights.

   Step 3. Receive the insights in front of your whole team, staying inside the five minutes to be efficient and targeted. Be sure to demonstrate the *3 Rs* as you receive your insights.

   Step 4. Highlight that regular sharing of insights with the whole team is a great way to reinforce openness and build trust.

4. After completing the demonstration, gain the team's agreement to trial the tool, then decide how often to repeat this as part of the team's operating rhythm.

Practice 3. Constructive challenging

Your ability to create an environment where team members feel safe to question, challenge and debate is crucial to a dynamic learning culture.

Chief Defence Scientist Professor Tanya Monro reinforces this approach: 'If we create enough psychological safety, then people actually call out what they see happening in a frank, respectful and constructive way.'

INSIGHT EXERCISE
Checklist for constructive challenging in teams

Use this activity to reflect on the quality and depth of constructive challenging in recent team meetings. The items and format can be used as a debriefing and discussion tool with your team at the end of a meeting. The rating scale is 1 - Never to 5 - Always.

Constructive challenging behaviours	1	2	3	4	5
Encouraged open debate without fear of retribution	o	o	o	o	o
Actively listened and acknowledged other points of view	o	o	o	o	o
Offered respectful and constructive feedback on proposals	o	o	o	o	o
Asked clarifying questions to gain a deeper understanding	o	o	o	o	o
Collaborated to find solutions to incorporate diverse perspectives	o	o	o	o	o

Go first

Creating a culture of innovation and adaptability requires you, as a leader, to actively encourage constructive challenging among team members. It's not just a nice-to-have; it's essential for achieving better decision making and outcomes. And the best way to foster this kind of culture is by setting an example. You must model the behaviour by asking questions and welcoming diverse viewpoints. By doing so, you demonstrate that conflict can be surfaced and dealt with in a safe space, giving team members the confidence to voice their opinions without fear of retribution.

Item B. Relentless debriefing

In any workplace environment learning needs to happen faster than the speed of change. When VUCA prevails, however, there is a very real risk of failure due to misaligned activity and lost opportunities.

When you need to drive team learning at pace, in high-demand environments, one tool stands out above all others: *the debrief.*

A debrief means reflecting (at any time) on how the team performed, then using the insights gained to rise to the next level. Regular, effective debriefing is a great way to boost teamwork and adaptability. It has many benefits, including boosting confidence and motivation by recognising and celebrating success, improving as a result of lessons learned, and addressing conflicts and concerns before they fester. It also helps to maintain standards and avoid repeating mistakes and encourages moving on from setbacks.

Let's address some of the basic steps to prepare for a debrief, then we'll introduce a primary tool, *Action debrief*, to provide a simple template from which you can innovate as the team gains more confidence and skill in debriefing.

Preparing to debrief

We covered the essentials of openness earlier in the chapter, so now we turn to setting up an effective debriefing process. The starting point for that is to choose the right attendees, time and venue and have your tool and process ready. For that we suggest the primary tool *Action debrief*.

Action debrief

The purpose of the *Action debrief* tool and accompanying canvas is to provide a step-by-step guide to the most basic of debriefing processes and templates. It assumes the debrief of an event, although the same process and template can apply to projects and general debriefing of progress.

INSTRUCTIONS

1. **Set the Debrief Stage:** Begin by clarifying the debrief goal and establish three team behaviour ground rules such as:

   » Cultivate curiosity for improvement.

   » Focus on learning, not blame.

   » Conclude with forward-looking perspectives.

2. **Canvas Setup:** Prepare the Action Debrief Canvas (overleaf) and proceed with the prompts in the following sections.

3. **Facilitation Steps:** During the process, guide the team as follows:

   » Encourage diverse viewpoints, staying fact-focused.

   » Utilise a whiteboard or equivalent to record and highlight the canvas data.

   » Extract valuable insights from both successes and setbacks.

   » Prioritise key takeaways and discuss their future application.

4. **Solidify Actions:** Conclude by establishing actionable steps using the 3 W's format:

   » What needs to be done?

   » Who will take responsibility?

   » When is the action set to occur?

Action Debrief Canvas

1 What was expected to happen?

Important goals, outcomes or milestones

Expected outputs and standards

Key behaviours and actions

Important context e.g. expected conditions

2 What actually happened?

Actual outcomes/results

Actual outputs and standards

Behaviours and actions or non-actions

Surprises or variations from the norm

3 What were the differences?

Met or exceeded expectations

Fell short of expectations

Contributors to these differences

Other observations about differences

4 How can we learn and improve?

Key lessons learned from the experience

Strengths to leverage or grow

Areas to develop or change

Important insights/future considerations

Facilitation guide

1. What was expected to happen?

Facilitate the team to develop a detailed list of what was expected to happen in this event including:

- » Important goals, outcomes and standards
- » Expected outputs and/or milestones
- » Key behaviours and actions

2. What actually happened?

Guide the team to discuss and reflect on what actually happened at each stage in the event. Consider outcomes achieved or missed, experiences and observed behaviours. Keep it factual and avoid problem solving or blaming. There will inevitably be opinions mixed in with facts, so make a note where there are differences of opinion. For example, people may have different views as to whether communication met expectations.

3. What were the differences?

Identify and record the differences between the expectations and what happened, including any surprises. Group items into:

- » Met expectations
- » Exceeded expectations
- » Fell short of expectations
- » Other

4. How can we learn and improve?

During the discussion about the differences between expectations and what happened use your facilitation skills to draw out constructive insights or actions. These may include potential reasons behind successes or setbacks and ideas for future improvement. Sort these into at least three categories:

- » How to capitalise on strengths and success
- » Needs and opportunities to learn and improve
- » Insights to be mindful of in the future

Mix it up

Be mindful to 'mix up' the style and timing of debriefing to keep it fresh and relevant. There are lots of alternatives to the standard debriefing tool, so use your imagination. Here is another simple format you may wish to use.

Debriefing questions

» What did we set out to achieve?

» What did we actually achieve?

» What worked well and why?

» Where could we learn and/or improve?

» What are the actions we want to take?

Make it a discipline

Discipline in debriefing is essential to promote team learning and adaptability. A regular commitment to reflect on events, projects and business cycles, to analyse outcomes and then to act on improvement is a key contributor to team performance. Anna Wenngren makes the case for debriefing as part of the performance cycle with three recommendations.

>   » Be transparent about what you want to accomplish.

>   » Give honest, compassionate feedback.

>   » Maintain a relentless focus on standards.

It is vital to approach debriefing with a relentless attitude, by consistently prioritising it despite the usual day-to-day pressures. This mindset is essential to make debriefing a regular practice that can drive continuous improvement and sustain performance even in turbulent times.

BUILDING BLOCK

6 Tempo

Establishing a deliberate tempo holds immense value for teams when the wider environment is unpredictable. It goes beyond reactivity and responsiveness, enabling them to synchronise efforts and operate in a more proactive and balanced way.

Navigation

The final part of the chapter focuses on tempo and introduces two important elements, *operating rhythm* and *delivering at pace*.

Operating rhythm refers to the routines and practices that help to align the team's activities with strategic goals and priorities. This is one of the most important team practices to establish and sustain in a changeable environment.

Delivering at pace draws on many concepts covered throughout this section and includes pinpointing specific challenges that can be impediments to agility and adaptability. At the end of the section we will summarise with an insight activity to reflect on your team's current readiness to operate in nonlinear conditions.

Item A. Disciplined operating rhythm

Operating rhythm is the cadence or tempo of your team's operations characterised by routines, rituals and practices. It's how you align activities (daily, weekly, quarterly) with strategic goals and priorities, put your plans into action and continuously review progress. It is the ACL in action, your 'navigation system' in turbulent times.

Some potential elements in that rhythm are highlighted in Figure 13.1.

An effective operating rhythm is particularly important in times of uncertainty because it reduces reactivity and ensures that key activities are performed in a consistent manner and to a high standard.

Find your ideal operating rhythm

The ideal operating rhythm is one that works for you, your team and your stakeholders.

Remember what Rebecca James advised in chapter 11: 'If you try to make promises to traditional cycles like three-year plans, you set your business up for rigidity, when what's needed is adaptability.'

That doesn't mean it will always be 'comfortable' or conventional, but it will help to instil balance and focus despite disruptions and multiple challenges.

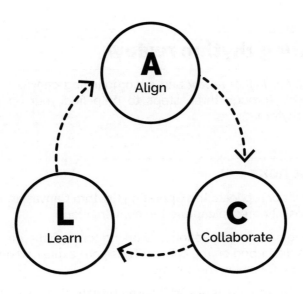

Align	Collaborate	Learn
Planning and budgeting	Meetings and forums	Monitoring and reviewing
Setting clear goals	Communicating	Renewing
Agreeing expectations	Problem solving	Reporting
Prioritising/ sequencing	Co-creating	Improving and adapting

Figure 13.1: elements of operating rhythm

Operating rhythm review

The *Operating rhythm review* and accompanying canvas is designed to guide you through three steps to help find your optimal team operating rhythm.

INSTRUCTIONS

1. Print or replicate the Operating Rhythm Canvas and use Post-it notes to capture the conversation.

2. Begin the conversation by working through the three steps as described on the canvas. These are explained on the page following the canvas.

    Step 1. Current and Desired Rituals. Create a list of activities repeated over time so you can define the rituals and routines for your operating rhythm (don't be limited by the canvas space because this can be a large set of items - so use the canvas steps as a prompt)

    Step 2. Principles and Standards. Draw out the important operating norms and principles that will shape your operating rhythm

    Step 3. Events, Activities, Rituals. Match the various events, activities and rituals to what they mean for team, people and stakeholders, such as performance and planning cycles

3. Be flexible and create whatever columns work best for you because the aim is to get a clear picture of the essential items in your operating rhythm, the time cycles and who they affect.

4. The outputs from this activity need to be refined and tested over time as you develop the operating rhythm that works best for your team. Expect adaptation, but be sure to keep the core disciplines in place and remember this is about a culture of learning and adapting as one team.

Operating Rhythm Canvas

1 Current and desired rituals

2 Principles and standards

3 Events, activities, rituals

Days	Team	People	Stakeholders
7			
30			
90			
360			

Using the Operating Rhythm Canvas

Step 1. Current and desired rituals

The first step is to create a list of current and desired activities that are repeated over time, with the goal of defining rituals and actions to be included in your operating rhythm. Include your current activities at this stage, then include any new activities suggested by your team (such as action debriefing of a key project). Here are some broad categories to stimulate your thinking.

Strategic and business planning	Meetings and forums	Communication and information flows	Financial planning and reporting
Governance reporting	Performance reporting	Human resources cycles	Stakeholder connection

Step 2. Principles and standards

The operating rhythm will be guided by operating norms and principles. For example, if you are strongly committed to agile ways of working, then some of those agile principles should be captured to ensure that the rhythm reflects those items and their intent. Alternatively, if you have natural segments like semesters in a university or governance cycles in a regulatory authority, then these should also help to shape your tempo.

Step 3. Events, activities, rituals

The canvas is laid out to consider and review the essential events, activities and rituals of your operating rhythm and what that means for your team, people and stakeholders. For example, the team column will likely include meetings and reporting, in the people column there will be performance management cycles, and for stakeholders possibly governance issues.

Be flexible and create whatever columns work best for you, but keep in mind that the aim is to get a clear picture of the essential items in your operating rhythm, the time cycles and who they affect.

REFLECT
Operating rhythm actions

- -

Building the Operating Rhythm Canvas provides an overall view of the key elements of team rhythm.

» What are your observations about the operating rhythm?

» Does it capture the key items?

» Is the tempo suitable and sustainable?

» Are there aspects to 'test and learn' to see if you can get greater value from the rhythm?

Item B. Deliver outcomes at pace

The final item on the Team Canvas describes delivering outcomes at pace through empowerment and accountability. It is a reminder that outcomes matter, as does the way they are achieved. Robert Iervasi: 'You might achieve your KPI or goal, but if the way you achieved it was to not take people on the journey, burn people along the way or cause disruption to the organisation, then the achievement of the outcome is acknowledged, but it doesn't mean it's a success.'

This is where earlier work on alignment and building a one team culture pay off. Andrew McConville: 'When you're aligned and unified by shared values and purpose, pressure brings a tighter bond. Trust each other, and together you'll weather the storm.'

Many of the tools covered in this section, such as *Team Diamond*, *Partnering Quadrant* and PROBED, will help to address those needs. It is also important to pinpoint and address three challenges facing advantage leaders when seeking pace, agility and one team behaviours:

Challenge 1	Challenge 2	Challenge 3
Delivering Sky to Ground	*Making tough calls on people*	*Saying no to pet projects*

Challenge 1. Delivering Sky to Ground

Organisations are complex and as a result they often create unhelpful tensions between functions that can directly inhibit pace and agility.

To deal with these tensions, we created the *Sky to Ground* model (see figure 13.2), which helps to highlight the very natural tensions between being efficient (delivering to plan) and at the same time being adaptable (creating and testing).

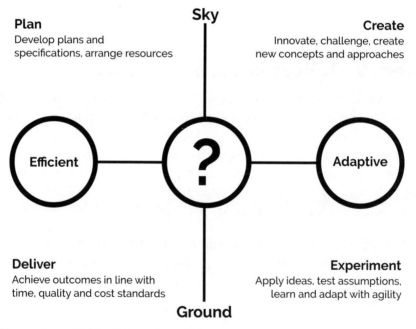

Plan
Develop plans and specifications, arrange resources

Sky

Create
Innovate, challenge, create new concepts and approaches

Efficient

?

Adaptive

Deliver
Achieve outcomes in line with time, quality and cost standards

Experiment
Apply ideas, test assumptions, learn and adapt with agility

Ground

Figure 13.2: Sky to Ground model

This model was originally developed to supplement the *Think One Team* method because enterprise leaders often spoke about the inherent dilemmas of balancing efficiency and adaptability. The question mark in the middle of the model is intended to provoke thinking and discussion about what draws these together, such as values, purpose or operating rhythm.

REFLECT
Sky to Ground

- -

» Do you recognise tensions between efficiency and adaptability in your organisation?

» What are the implications of those tensions?

» What fits in the middle of the model for your organisation?

Challenge 2. Making tough calls on people

For reasons of confidentiality, we won't share specific stories or quotes from advantage leaders on this topic. Most, however, emphasised the importance and challenge of making tough calls on people.

Time and again from these leaders and others across our network we have heard the sentiment, *I wish I'd made the decision earlier to move them on* or *I'm still struggling to make the call.*

It can be reassuring to know that even the most experienced senior leaders find these people decisions particularly difficult. It can offer a false sense of comfort to delay what you know is the right thing to do. Research shows that while we experience regret for the decision in the short term, it is the inaction, the 'error of omission', that actually generates more regret in the long run.

HOW TO LEAN INTO THE TOUGH PEOPLE DECISIONS

The word 'decision' derives from the Latin word *caedere* meaning 'to cut off', which is a reminder that when you do make that tough call you cut off potential futures irrespective of whether the person leaves or stays. If they leave, you've cut them off from the team; if they stay, you've cut off other possible futures.

There are many ways to assess the performance potential of your team members, and no doubt you will have data from sources such as performance agreements, 360-degree feedback and regular observations.

To supplement that data here's a straightforward, honest reflection exercise to complete yourself or with your coach to assess whether each member of your team is still 'fit for purpose'.

INSIGHT EXERCISE
Fit for purpose

Jot down the names of each member of your team and consider the following questions about each of them:

» Are you 100 per cent confident they will be a top performer over the next 6–18 months? If yes, refer to the coaching tools later in the book to support and stretch them.

» If no, what precisely is the gap you see between their current performance and what is needed from a top performer? Is it more about task or people issues?

» Are you certain they can be coached or developed to bridge the gap at pace so there will be minimal negative business impact?

» If no, would you recruit this person now if the position was open, and if so why?

» If these questions lead you to seriously question whether it makes sense to continue with them, then what is stopping you from making that call now? Will the short-term regret be worth the longer-term benefits?

When you apply this assessment and reach the conclusion that one or more members of your team are no longer fit for purpose, then you do them and your organisation no favours by avoiding the decision. Remember, making the tough call doesn't mean you can't be respectful, caring and empathetic. It's what advantage leadership is all about.

Challenge 3. Saying no to pet projects

People naturally develop preferences for projects or initiatives based on personal interest, expertise, strategic alignment, or the investment of time and effort.

This can be problematic in a world that is changing fast and in unpredictable ways, which is why we believe that one of Martin's favourite edicts — 'Just because it was strategic yesterday does not mean it is today' — should be stamped on the strategic and operational plans of every team, no matter when they were authored.

Everything needs to be regularly reviewed and challenged to ensure it is relevant in the changing conditions. This includes your own pet projects!

REFLECT
Alertness to change

    »   What does Martin's edict mean for you and your team?

    »   Which of yesterday's strategies or projects need to be revisited?

    »   How do you create the habits within yourself and your team to be relentlessly alert for these changes?

There's no doubt this exercise requires 'embracing the squirm'. However, we close with a thought from Marie Kondo:

> To truly cherish the things that are important to you, you must first discard those that have outlived their purpose. And if you no longer need them, then that is neither wasteful nor shameful.

Rigidity or agility?

All the concepts and tools in this book are intended to develop agility and adaptability in your ways of thinking and working, and in doing so allow you to create and build effective teams that learn at pace and adapt to the impacts of turbulence.

Accordingly, we conclude this chapter with an insight exercise that encourages you to reflect on whether the prevailing mindset and ways of working of your team are oriented more to a linear or a nonlinear environment.

INSIGHT EXERCISE
Linear vs nonlinear approach

The items on the left-hand side are better suited to a linear environment (stable, predictable), whereas those on the right are better suited to a nonlinear environment (changeable, complex). Reflect on where your team is currently positioned between the items, and where you want them to be. Consider introducing this exercise to your team to provoke thinking and challenging about ways of working. It is yet another step in making team learning a habit.

We are problem solvers	—	We are solution seekers
We like to plan each step in advance	—	We like a clear outcome and then we iterate
We expect senior leaders to make decisions	—	We are empowered to make decisions
We work in functional units and hierarchy	—	We work across functions and hierarchy
We plan to avoid risk and failure	—	We act to rapidly test, learn and adapt

We rely on individuals to take the lead	—	We lead through small, fast, empowered teams
We budget and work in mid- to long-term cycles	—	We budget and work in short sprints
We meet to share information	—	We meet to share achievements and problem solve

Recap

In uncertain and disrupted environments, open, agile and adaptable teams have a significant advantage because they learn quickly and make adjustments on the run.

These capabilities require teams to be open to feedback and to relentlessly debrief. That helps them to identify what's working and what's not, and to make changes quickly. A disciplined operating rhythm is essential for a team to act in this way because it provides a predictable 'drumbeat' for learning and realigning when conditions change. This rhythm helps a team sustain momentum and deliver results without being overly reactive or trapped in short-term thinking.

By embracing these tools and practices, you can foster a culture of empowerment and accountability within your team where people are open to learning and improving. In doing so, you will create a shared sense of ownership for achieving success. In turn, this will enable you to navigate even the most turbulent of environments with confidence and agility.

Learnings

» To **learn** is to be open, agile and adaptable (for a purpose). This will ensure your team is equipped to navigate the pace and challenges of a disruptive, nonlinear environment.

» **Reflection** and **feedback** are essential for personal growth and for helping your team avoid blind spots, which can be showstoppers in fast-changing conditions.

» Constructive **challenging** of each other's ideas and assumptions is the cornerstone of effective debating and decision making, particularly when issues are complex and adaptive.

» First **seek** feedback or **insights** before offering them to others

» In a changeable environment the best teams use relentless and intensive **debriefing** to deliberately and frequently 'close the loop'.

» **Operating rhythm** creates a team tempo to allow you to navigate and deliver in turbulent times.

5

Coach

*... be the coach
your people need*

In Part 4 you learned about the **blueprint for teamwork** and the **Team Canvas**. Then you explored a range of tools to guide your team to **align**, **collaborate** and **learn**. In this part the focus is on one core message: **be the coach your people need**. You will learn how to unlock potential by **putting people first**, making **vulnerability** a strength, then reimagining the **performance conversation**. This will equip you with tools to build strong coaching relationships with the people you lead.

CHAPTER 14

Be the coach your people need

*What does 'be the coach your people need' mean?
What is the superpower of the best coaches? How
do you build a coaching relationship? What tools
do coaches use to create the environment for
performance and wellbeing.*

Unlocking potential

On a hot Dubai afternoon a few years ago Graham watched as Ashley
Ross, Head Coach of the International Cricket Council Academy, led 30
coaches onto the beautifully manicured oval.

It was the opening of the Global Coaches Program, and instead of the
anticipated speech he divided them into groups of three and gave each
group a medicine ball and a few plastic cups.

'Please place a cup on the oval 50 metres away from the medicine
ball,' he instructed them to quizzical looks, before asking each group
to nominate one person as coach, one as a player, and the other to use
their phone to video the coaching to follow.

'Players, your objective is to crush the cup by landing the medicine ball
on top of the cup in the fewest possible throws. You can't walk with the
ball, you must do it safely, and you have a coach to help you. Everything
the coach does including instructions, feedback and tone will be
videoed.' That was it. No other instructions.

Suddenly coaches sprang into action. Some picked up a medicine ball and demonstrated throwing techniques; others asked players about their plans; still others stood back and wondered what this was all about.

Twenty minutes later there were many crushed cups, lots of laughter and some remarkable videos of diverse coaching styles.

Fast forward a week to the end of the program and everyone was watching a crush-the-cup video and critiquing their coaching approach.

Amongst much embarrassment, one universal theme emerged, best described by an experienced Sri Lankan coach: 'I think we've switched from thinking that a coach has to have all the answers to seeing our purpose is to unlock the potential in the player.'

In sport, and more recently in business, the quest to nurture and unlock potential has supplanted the 'coach-as-expert' who previously saw their role as extracting performance like juice from a lemon.

The modern coach guides, supports, challenges and mentors individual team members and the whole team to unlock their potential, especially in turbulent conditions.

Three shifts in approach

Three differences in mindset and behaviours distinguish the traditional role of coach from this new approach, and they offer a guide for advantage leaders in how to strengthen coaching skills and impact.

Role	**to**	Relationship
Clever	**to**	Curious
Technical	**to**	Adaptable

» *Role to Relationship* is the big shift. The new coach is more approachable, transparent, and responsive to people's needs and concerns. Their communication is two way and decisions are shared. Ashley Ross observes, 'It's about the people being coached, having real trust that the coach is there for them and that they do care.'

» *Clever to Curious* means the coach is no longer the instructor with all the answers; instead they ask lots of questions to encourage a growth mindset and to help capture valuable insights.

» *Technical to Adaptable* signals the shift from teacher of technical know-how to facilitator of learning and adaptability. The coach provokes, challenges and guides to unlock and unblock potential.

REFLECT
Your coaching mindset

Based on the descriptions of the three shifts, how do you believe others would view your approach to coaching in the workplace?

Role	O	O	O	O	O	**Relationship**
Clever	O	O	O	O	O	**Curious**
Technical	O	O	O	O	O	**Adaptable**

Guiding principles to 'be the coach'

Underpinning the shift towards relationship, curiosity and adaptability are three fundamental coaching principles seen in the habits of effective coaches and integral to developing coaching skills and capabilities:

1. Put people first.

2. Make vulnerability a strength.

3. Reimagine the performance conversations.

Why are these three principles so important? Prioritising people is essential to creating a supportive and empowering environment built on individual needs, motivations and aspirations. Embracing vulnerability as a strength helps coaches to foster trust, authenticity and connection, establishing the space for open dialogue and growth. Additionally, performance conversations are the pivotal opportunity for coaches to transform mindsets and behaviours.

Let's explore each and add some new tools to your toolkit to help you become the coach your people need.

Coaching principle 1. Put people first

SEEK was rated as Australia's Best Place to Work in 2021, and one of Australia's Top Ten Places to Work in Technology in 2022 and 2023, so it's no surprise when CFO Kate Koch shares, 'My core job is to be available to support my team and ensure that they have the resources they need to succeed. I have learned to be more ruthless in delegating tasks to which I personally can add little value and changing my mindset about these interactions. By empowering and supporting my team, they are more motivated to get things done and we get a better outcome.'

Putting people first is a winning strategy for advantage leaders. Martin describes it like this: 'Always focus first on people, with task following close behind.'

Figure 14.1 offers some handy examples to reflect on your own leadership style. It may also offer broader insights into the leadership culture of your organisation.

Put people last	Put people second	Put people first
Ignore wellbeing	Focus just on getting tasks done	Prioritise wellbeing
Discourage creativity		Actively listen to people's needs
Dismiss input from employees	Push people to their limits	Encourage collaboration
Allow bullying or harassment	Disregard morale	Provide growth opportunities
Fail to provide resources	Value productivity over people	Show empathy and understanding
Don't acknowledge good work	Ignore personal struggles	Say thank you and recognise effort
	Micromanage and instruct	

Figure 14.1: people first

REFLECT
People first

- » Based on the items in the table, how would you rate your commitment to putting people first?
- » Where are your strengths?
- » Would you be a better coach by embracing one or more of the people-first behaviours?

It's your choice

People first seems an obvious strategy, because employees who feel valued, heard and supported are more likely to be committed and engaged. So why do many leaders and organisations put people second or last?

Sometimes it's lack of awareness or skills. The pressure to deliver on targets often drives leaders to prioritise tasks over people. For others, it can be wariness or mistrust, a belief this approach will not lead to better outcomes.

The people-first choice is exactly that, a choice. It doesn't so much require a new tool as an awareness of your current leadership style and willingness to experiment with new behaviours, such as those described in figure 14.1.

How do you boost that awareness? Start with considering if your natural tendency is to think 'people first' or 'task first'. Task first isn't inherently wrong. For example, in a crisis it's often absolutely crucial, as Kevin Sullivan demonstrated when keeping QF72 in the air. In most situations it's important to be goal oriented and practical in your decision making.

Be aware of how others experience your task-first thinking. Does it mean you exclude them from decisions, fail to show empathy for their hopes and concerns, or plan for things but not for people? Subtle changes in the way you engage with people alongside the tasks that need to be done can have big positive effects.

Coaching principle 2. Make vulnerability a strength

Vulnerability for a leader is the readiness to openly and authentically share personal experiences and emotions with others.

This topic goes right to the heart of shedding protective and defensive behaviour. The sheer weight of comments from advantage leaders regarding a change in vulnerability stands out as the biggest shift we have observed in mindset and approach. It was such a dominant theme that it could have been a feature in several places in the book. We chose the coaching section, however, because we believe vulnerability in the way you coach people is an essential ingredient in bringing your toolkit for turbulence to life.

Once again, it's important to highlight how the pandemic was an accelerant for change. This time it's about the vulnerability of leaders.

Instead of office-based relationships, work colleagues were literally beamed into each other's homes, and as a result personal barriers dissolved in ways that surprised even the most empathetic and deliberately vulnerable leaders.

Paul Duldig: 'I always thought of myself as someone who had that openness and vulnerability, but the change in magnitude was huge and extremely positive on both sides.

'In the past there was a reasonably clear line between what's work, what's not work. Then that line kept moving, and you start asking yourself, "Well actually, what's the purpose of the line?" I realised it was the generous and right thing to do to just be available to support people, and one way to do that was to be totally open about my own feelings and experience.'

Why vulnerability matters

Vulnerability helps to build authentic and genuine connections and relationships, and creates a safe and supportive environment. That's fertile ground for the openness and risk taking needed to tackle tough problems and learn together.

Ashley Ross, who has trained business leaders and coached world-class teams in men's and women's sport, observes: 'In our culture vulnerability has often been seen as a weakness; however, it's far more a strength, particularly for a coach, because you normalise the experience of errors and learning.'

Seven signs of vulnerability

When asked how he had changed as a person to help build the trust, respect and connection people want and need from leaders in a high-growth, high-demand setting, Brett Wickham was succinct: 'I'd characterise it in one word, vulnerability.'

Advantage leaders demonstrate seven distinct signs of vulnerability. Each is underpinned by emotional openness, and these signs provide an excellent model and tool to reflect on current practices, and to identify opportunities to strengthen this game-changing attribute.

It is important to stress that vulnerability with your team isn't necessarily the same as in other situations, such as with a strategic partner or Board.

We asked Ashley Ross, what is the point at which vulnerability can shift from being a strength to a weakness for a coach?

'There's obviously a limit to expressing your failures and vulnerability,' he replied. 'And it's that point where the vulnerability starts to erode confidence in the leader rather than helping to foster connection.'

This is a useful distinction and one to keep in mind as we explore each of the seven signs vulnerability.

1. ADMIT UNCERTAINTY

While the conventional leader wants to show they are the expert and in control, an advantage leader is willing to say they don't know and to admit their uncertainty about decisions. Kevin Sullivan continued to lead his crew and the arriving rescue authorities as he stood amongst the passengers of QF72 and, when asked, admitted he didn't know what had happened to the plane. That didn't make him weaker; it demonstrated his honesty. He didn't give away power in that situation; instead he gained more trust and respect.

2. BE OPEN TO FEEDBACK

Leaders who seek and welcome feedback demonstrate vulnerability, and this helps to create a culture of trust and openness to take risks and learn. Feedback isn't just about one-to-one performance conversations; it's also about a culture of transparency and openness. Anna Wenngren: 'With all staff we communicate our financial position, where we need to get to and the timeframes around when we want to get there. That means totally open Q&As so people can ask the leadership team absolutely anything about that.'

3. ASK FOR HELP

Leaders who ask for help or seek guidance show humility and a willingness to learn. That encourages others to do the same, an essential ingredient in environments where everyone is 'learning on the fly'. Andrew McConville: 'It's having the confidence and in many ways the vulnerability to not see yourself as needing to be the expert.'

4. SHOW EMOTIONS

The traditional role of leader has been to be more formal and guarded, but that too has changed, as Robert Iervasi shares: 'What I learned during COVID-19 was to remove some of the formality in the way that I was engaging and communicating and to share how I was feeling. It was a way of demonstrating that, as a group, we were all in there together.'

5. SHARE STORIES

We are wired to respond to stories, and when leaders share their experiences of struggles and challenges it makes them more authentic and helps to show understanding and build empathy. Kate Koch: 'I spend a lot more time having deeper-level conversations or ask-me-anything sessions where nothing is left on the table.'

6. ADMIT MISTAKES

Admitting mistakes shows honesty and openness to learning and growing from imperfections. It can also deepen relationships and create opportunities for support and understanding from others. Chris Tanti: 'I want to set the example. I want us to be able to talk about our mistakes, learn from our mistakes, not feel bad about them, because I still want people to stretch themselves, and people aren't going to stretch themselves if they're worried about being ridiculed.'

7. TAKE RISKS

The final of the seven signs is about calculated risk taking and stepping outside your comfort zone. Leaning into the unknown helps you to shape and challenge paradigms and practices and by doing so you can be more at ease with being vulnerable. Earlier in the book we shared Sally Capp's remarkable courage to front the media and say, 'I got it wrong.' Asked what difference that has made in her approach to leadership, she replied, 'I am open to failure and risk more than ever before and owning the mistakes,' which, as we know, is a key to navigating complex problems.

The primary tool *Seven signs of vulnerability* will help to boost awareness of vulnerability as a foundation for being the coach your people need.

Seven signs of vulnerability

Vulnerability is readiness to openly and authentically share personal experiences and emotions with others. It is a powerful way to build trust with the people you lead and to set the foundation for being the coach your people need.

INSTRUCTIONS

1. Familiarise yourself with each of the seven signs and their associated behaviours.

2. Complete the self-evaluation on the next page and share the results with someone whose opinion you trust.

3. Keep a copy of the model handy as a reference to remind you of the seven signs.

4. Choose one sign of vulnerability to improve and model the thinking and behaviours in your interactions with your team.

5. Reflect on what effect that small change in habit has on you and on the people you lead.

1 Admit uncertainty
Say you don't know.
Admit to an uncertain decision.

2 Open to feedback
Ask for feedback.
Graciously accept critiquing.

3 Ask for help
Ask others' opinions.
Ask for support.

4 Show emotions
Express your feelings.
Let your guard down.

5 Share stories
Tell about struggles.
Tell about challenges.

6 Admit mistakes
Take responsibility.
Acknowledge a stuff up.

7 Take risks
Take a calculated risk.
Do something uncomfortable.

INSIGHT TOOL
Seven signs of vulnerability — self-evaluation

Complete the self-evaluation then ask a trusted colleague to provide their reflection on your assessment. Keep the model *Seven signs of vulnerability* visible as you act on any insights to boost your vulnerability as a leader and coach.

SEVEN SIGNS OF VULNERABILITY	Area to improve	Acceptable	Strength to sustain
1. Admit uncertainty			
Say you don't know	O	O	O
Admit to uncertainty about decisions	O	O	O
2. Open to feedback			
Ask for feedback	O	O	O
Graciously accept critiquing	O	O	O
3. Ask for help			
Ask others' opinions	O	O	O
Ask for support	O	O	O

(continued)

SEVEN SIGNS OF VULNERABILITY	Area to improve	Acceptable	Strength to sustain
4. Show emotions			
Express your feelings	O	O	O
Let your guard down	O	O	O
5. Share stories			
Tell others about struggles	O	O	O
Tell others about challenges	O	O	O
6. Admit mistakes			
Take responsibility	O	O	O
Acknowledge a mistake	O	O	O
7. Take risks			
Take a calculated risk	O	O	O
Do something uncomfortable	O	O	O

Coaching principle 3. Reimagine the performance conversations

In the emotional roller coaster of turbulence, the best coaches invariably ramp up their one-to-one conversations with their team.

There are many reasons for this, but arguably the most important is that people are unique individuals and experience turbulence in different ways. At any given moment some will be on top of their tasks, feeling calm and in control, while others may be feeling overwhelmed, isolated and out of control.

Martin observes, 'One of the biggest learnings and development areas for me from COVID-19 was how to build a deeper one-to-one relationship with each of my team so I could be an effective coach.'

To equip and support Martin we had to address one inconvenient truth, then redesign the way he interacted with his team so he had the tools to be the coach they needed.

The inconvenient truth

While organisations invest extraordinary amounts of time and money on performance management systems, the reality is that the tools and associated methods are built on principles and assumptions from the industrial age, and are certainly not attuned with *people first* or *make vulnerability a strength*.

The feedback cycle times are too slow, the process reinforces hierarchical status, and the support tools tend to overly prioritise individual performance while missing other important aspects such as wellbeing and teamwork. This is not the way to build a trust-based coaching relationship!

Performance partnering

Some years ago Graham developed an innovative way to change the dynamics of performance conversation practices between leaders and their team members. That approach, called *performance partnering*, didn't alter the organisation's performance management process but instead focused on equipping leaders with practical tools to transform those conversations. Three core principles defined this new approach:

» **Redefine performance.** Talk about the real contributors to sustainable high performance.

» **Make it a partnership.** Replace the traditional boss to subordinate thinking.

» **Loop and learn together.** Apply a relevant and disciplined tempo to suit the context.

VCE were trained in performance partnering the year before COVID-19, so we just needed to accelerate and deepen the way it was used.

Let's explain a little more about this process, the principles that underpin it and how you can apply it with your team.

Principle 1.	Principle 2.	Principle 3.
Redefine performance	*Make it a partnership*	*Loop and learn together*

Performance partnering principle 1. Redefine performance

For most people, and in most workplace systems, 'performance' means achieving goals or performance standards, and perhaps other items such as training and development priorities and behaviours linked to values.

While those are important, the frame is too narrow to address the real inputs to sustaining high performance in fast-changing and volatile conditions.

Performance partnering starts with a better definition of performance, broken into four essential elements:

» **A**chievement — of meaningful outcomes

» **D**evelopment — of new skills, knowledge and capabilities

» **E**njoyment — by gaining positive energy

» **P**artnering — by forging trust-based relationships

These four crucial elements in sustaining performance provide an excellent framework, which is shown in the primary tool *Understand the ADEP model*.

Understand the ADEP model

The ADEP model illustrates the four key elements that sustain high performance. These are used in the primary tool *Performance partnering* and as a guide for ongoing coaching of team members. This tool is intended as a way to personally familiarise yourself with the ADEP elements before engaging with your team.

INSTRUCTIONS

1. Familiarise yourself with the brief guide to each of the four ADEP elements that follows.

2. Practise using the ADEP model by printing or sketching the ADEP 90-Day Canvas and using the prompts to reflect on your aims for the next 90 days. Choose whether to focus the ADEP specifically on work and career or to extend to all parts of your life.

3. Keep the 90-day aims and plans in mind as you learn and apply the ADEP model in the upcoming primary tool *Performance partnering* with each of the people you lead.

A brief guide to the ADEP elements

To support your own planning and to familiarise yourself with the ADEP model before performance partnering conversations with your team, here are basic definitions of each of the ADEP elements and examples of the topics that will likely be part of your thinking and conversations. Read these before using the canvas.

Achieve is about meaningful outcomes, because we are all wired to gain satisfaction from achieving things that matter. This means considering aspirations such as long-term vision, purpose, important goals and priorities, together with standards of quality and excellence. Achievement of milestones and overall success are at the heart of this element.

Develop is about growth in skills, knowledge and capabilities. Your plans and conversations in this element might include fostering a growth mindset, capitalising on strengths, learning from experiences, training, and finding new and better ways.

Enjoy is about positive energy. Plans and conversations might address what brings stimulation and joy, how to sustain personal wellbeing and resilience, finding a constructive environment to trigger the blue zone, and cultivating an optimistic mindset.

Partner is about forging trust-based relationships and includes connecting and collaborating, communication style preferences, resolving unhelpful conflicts, supporting others and being team oriented. When reflecting on this element take time to consider your most important relationships and what is needed to build and sustain trust and connection.

When you have applied the ADEP model to your own plans and actions we turn to using it as a guide to establishing expectations with your individual team members, to debriefing the agreed performance cycles and to framing ongoing coaching conversations.

ADEP 90-Day Canvas

 Achieve

List your 3–5 most important goals for the next 90 days.

 Develop

Identify the most important thing to get better at in the next 90 days to be a more effective leader. Define your action plan.

 Enjoy

Define three specific actions to build and sustain your positive mental and physical energy in the next 90 days.

 Partner

Identify two important relationships to strengthen in the next 90 days. Define your plan for each.

ADEP is sustainable

ADEP is a much more balanced and sustainable way to describe, discuss and manage personal and team performance. The acronym ADEP has become the popular way to capture the associated process, which now features in many of Australia's leading universities, technology companies, banks and government agencies.

Martin explains, 'ADEP became one of my most important tools for managing in turbulent times because everything depended on supporting my team through those four aspects. This gave us a framework everyone understood, liked and found valuable even in the toughest of times.'

We will show you how to use ADEP as the primary tool (framework) for aligning expectations with your team members, and to use it as a frame for coaching on a day-to-day basis.

Performance partnering principle 2. Make it a partnership

The second principle of performance partnering is to build a partnering relationship between the leader and each person they lead. This relationship is arguably the most important partnership in any organisation. Of course, the concept of 'partnership' is quite different from the traditional idea of a 'boss' and their 'direct report' and therefore requires openness and trust.

Why is that important? Because, as coaching expert Ashley Ross observes, 'Engagement and development occur at the pace of trust.'

And, Martin adds, 'Without trust I couldn't give my team the emotional support they needed, so a partnering relationship was the key to unlocking their ability to sustain the ADEP performance.'

REFLECT

Boss or partner?

- -

Take a few moments to consider what it means to establish partnering relationships with your team, and perhaps with your leader.

» What do you believe are the characteristics of a partnering relationship?

» What implications does this relationship have for you as leader and for your people?

» How can you approach performance partnering to give it the greatest opportunity of success?

Performance partnering principle 3. Learn and loop together

Advantage leaders are already using 'loop and learn' principles to guide the team operating rhythm (ACL), so the one-to-one conversations are just another part of that rhythm.

The process is simple:

» Every 90 days you prepare and meet with each of your team members to discuss and agree on the priorities in each ADEP area for the 90 days ahead.

» You check in regularly on progress (about every 30 days), then debrief and reset at 90 days.

» Use the ADEP framework to guide your coaching approach with each individual.

Martin's description of how he used this approach will give you a clear view of what is possible.

ADEP and performance partnering in action

Martin recalls exactly how he got started with ADEP.

I remember Graham introducing ADEP to me and my team in a workshop environment well in advance of the pandemic. Like all teams we had some partnering issues, so the model immediately grabbed my attention. I was also frustrated that my team were not prioritising their own development and enjoyment, despite my best efforts through our traditional performance management processes. I could immediately see how the ADEP process would allow me to tee up those conversations and shift my role to coach rather than manager.

I agreed with my team that we would give it a go and once every 90 days schedule an ADEP conversation. I asked them to complete the ADEP Canvas with a look back to the prior 90 days and a look forward to the 90 days ahead. We linked Achieve to their existing objectives, but I encouraged them to add other achievements that mattered to them. Allowing them that moment of pause and reflection every 90 days proved to be very powerful, particularly where it created the space for open and honest conversations, I guess it encouraged us both to be more vulnerable.

ADEP quickly became our shorthand for a very different type of conversation, and we learned to have them on a regular basis outside of the 90-day structure. Once COVID-19 hit, this became very important as I had to up the pace to weekly, and at times daily, ADEP conversations. As I look back, I know it helped us tackle some potential team-threatening partnering issues, to maintain shape and wellbeing, and to stay focused on constantly learning and developing while we battled the impact of COVID-19 and beyond.

Let's use the primary tool *Performance partnering* to help you create and sustain a stronger coaching relationship with your individual team members.

Performance partnering

Use the *Performance partnering* tool and accompanying canvas with each of the people you lead to set the foundation for the coaching relationship and to guide your coaching tempo.

INSTRUCTIONS

1. Download (from www.toolkitforturbulence.com), print or reproduce copies of the Performance Partnering Canvas for yourself and each individual team member. Also review the guide points overleaf.

2. Confirm the tempo you intend to use. For example, the default is a 90-day cycle with 30-day check-ins.

   Step 1: Prepare. Arrange a time for the initial performance partnering conversations and ensure that you and each individual prepare your thoughts based on the prompts on the canvas.

   Step 2: Align. Hold the individual meetings, and discuss and confirm the top ADEP priorities. Be sure not to include too many and make them specific so you will both know when they have been reached.

   Step 3: Check in. Catch up at the agreed times and every 90 days do a full debrief and reset for the next 90 days.

Performance Partnering Canvas

Step 1
Prepare

Be prepared to have a conversation where you both reflect on the previous cycle and share and align on the ADEP for the next cycle.

Step 2
Align

Discuss and confirm the top priorities in each of the ADEP areas for the next cycle.

Achieve
The most important goals/milestones in the next cycle

Enjoy
How to sustain energy, wellbeing and satisfaction

Develop
Development of skills, knowledge and capabilities

Partner
Important relationships and connections to build or sustain

Step 3
Check in

Take time to reflect on progress, setbacks and insights.

Insights looking back ...

Insights to apply ...

Guide to the performance partnering steps

The canvas describes the three core steps; however, these guide points will support you to get the performance partnering process flowing for your team.

Key points in each ADEP item

For steps 1 and 2 on the canvas, following is a guide to the type of items to build into the conversation:

Achieve

Consider what success means and the specific goals and priorities to include in the Performance Plan for the next cycle. Beware of choosing too many items. See if you can clearly describe what 'done' means for each item — that may quite possibly be progress milestones and not completion.

Develop

This includes skills, knowledge and capabilities that are important to develop for the role, together with aspirations for career and future.

Reflect on one or two specific areas to develop in the next performance cycle. Include the actions required to make the positive change.

Enjoy

Consider what makes work enjoyable and energising, such as being challenged or working in a team environment. Consider values or principles that are really important. You might explore non-work items here but that's a personal choice. Also touch on the things that deplete energy.

Partner

Reflect on preferred ways to communicate, deal with problems and work together. Talk about how to set each other up for success in the next cycle and include a discussion about other partnering relationships that are important and need to be strengthened or sustained.

Choose the tempo

The performance partnering tempo provides focus and consistency in a fast-changing and adaptive environment.

The default tempo is 90 days, although this will vary depending on your context. We have seen the best results when leaders and their people have a check-in approximately every 30 days and a review and reset for the next cycle approximately every 90 days.

At these catch-ups the agenda is guided by the check-in frame in step 3 of the canvas.

Make ADEP your coaching frame

Performance partnering is a powerful tool for establishing and sustaining a coaching relationship with your team members. By defining performance (ADEP), building trust through partnerships and creating a loop-and-learn structure, you can better support, guide and challenge your team members.

As Martin explained, the structure provided by the ADEP framework provides an ideal basis for regular coaching conversations.

This method is now used widely across a vast range of organisations as a supplement to standard performance management processes and, more importantly, to transform the relationship between leaders and the people they lead.

The introduction here equips you to put the basic steps in place to test and learn how ADEP can add positive value in your team and organisation. Further support and training can be accessed from the website.

Learnings

» A coach **unlocks the potential** of the people they coach and that's what people need from their leaders in uncertain and changeable times.

» Modern coaches have shifted their approach from **role to relationship**, **clever to curious** and **technical to adaptable**; it's about caring and creating an environment of trust where people are open to learn and grow.

» A key to being the coach your people need is to **'put people first'**. That means prioritising wellbeing, being attentive and empathetic, helping them grow and acknowledging their efforts.

» Embrace the **ADEP** model as a tool to align expectations, check in on performance and guide your ongoing coaching.

» **Performance partnering** is a practical and proven way to reimagine the performance conversation and to create the foundation for a coaching relationship.

» Establish a **partnering relationship** with the people you lead.

» **Loop and learn** together to coach and guide your people to be the best they can be.

6

Scale

... for life, team and enterprise

In Part 5 you learned about the mindset and skills of a **coach**, and models such as **ADEP** that provide tools for you to unlock potential. In this final part we focus on helping you choose the **highest priority tools** to include in your toolkit for turbulence. The tools you select may be used for personal performance and wellbeing, to make you a more effective advantage leader, or to guide your team to be the best they can be. There is also potential to **lift your sights** to enhance leadership and team capability across your enterprise. You are an advantage leader; you have a toolkit that can turn disruption to advantage. Is it time to play a **bigger game?**

CHAPTER 15
Turn adversity to your advantage

We've shown you how leaders across a vast array of industries and workplaces have turned the shock, upheaval and uncertainty of disruption into advantage by supercharging their adaptability.

We've given you the mental models, the language, the tools and we hope the inspiration to be an advantage leader. It's important to recognise that leadership development is a journey and there is much still to do, because advantage leaders build and adapt enduring habits over time.

The application of the *Toolkit for Turbulence* isn't limited to you as a leader and your team, although that has been our primary focus in this book. Every aspect of life is being impacted by the forces of turbulence: new technologies, economic pressures, never-ending political conflict, societal shifts, environmental imperatives and so on. Much of what is contained in this book can be applied to aspects of your life outside of work, and we encourage you to apply them wherever you need to lead and influence others.

At the opening of most chapters, we posed a series of questions. We invite you to take the time to revisit those questions now. They are important in helping you choose your foundation habits and tools: those that you will carry every day in your leadership toolkit.

To guide you as you develop your own toolkit, we provide you with a snapshot of the six parts of the book in figure 15.1, followed by summaries of the key content in each part and a collated list of the primary tools.

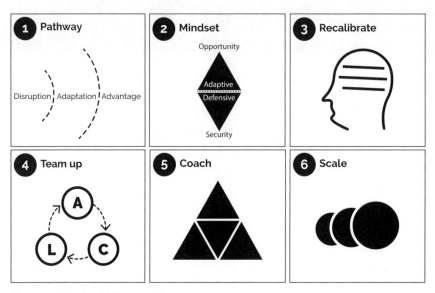

Figure 15.1: toolkit overview

Toolkit summaries

Each part of the book has a core message to help you choose and build your foundation habits and select the tools to go with them. The great thing about a toolkit is that you know where it is, you know what's inside and you know which tool to use when you have something to work on. That's how we want you to use this book. Review the summaries, scan the list of primary tools and canvases and use them as a prompt to guide your thinking as you develop a plan for you, your team and your enterprise to thrive in these turbulent times.

Part 1. Pathway

Business leaders across the world are facing once-in-a-lifetime turbulence: pandemic; inflation, cyber-attacks, environmental risks; workforce shortages, supply chain disruption; social media 'storms', government policy changes; capital crunch; energy costs, hybrid working and generative AI. Conventional 'leadership playbooks' and ways of working have been rendered obsolete by this nonlinear world and many leaders feel exposed, overwhelmed and fatigued, at a time when they need all the energy, skill and capability they can muster.

Amidst the volatility and confusion are leaders who have taken a different approach. Instead of bunkering down they have stepped into the storm.

Leaders like Andrew McConville, who advises, 'You've got to confront the reality that you're in a turbulent environment and then work out your key tools to get through that, because turbulence is inevitable.'

These are advantage leaders, and *Toolkit for Turbulence* tells their stories to inspire, equip and support you to apply the mindset, methods and tools to turn adversity to advantage.

The Pathway model captured the essence of the advantage leaders' approach, although certainly the nature of disruption varies enormously from one workplace to another.

In the technology sector adversity has been financial, while in aged care the pandemic continues. In the energy sector rapid growth drives the need to adapt; manufacturing faces inflation and supply chain disruption; universities confront generative AI alongside business model challenges; and every tier of government faces the relentless demand of more from less.

Whatever the disruption, advantage leaders have applied similar principles: seeing creative opportunities in adversity; using it as a 'force multiplier' to motivate and accelerate the growth of new adaptive capabilities in themselves and their teams; and giving them, their team and their enterprise the advantage of being versatile enough to emerge stronger from any type of disruption.

Three takeaways are immediately important for your toolkit:

» **Be inspired.** The stories of Captains Sullivan and Sullenberger remind us that when confronted with unprecedented challenges it is time to toss aside conventional wisdom and, in the moment, cobble together the tools we need to avert disaster.

» **Expect turbulence.** The disruption may vary but just as no one was immune to the pandemic, there is no end in sight to the wave upon wave of challenge and change from technology, the environment, social movements and the global economy.

» **Step out on the pathway.** Take the three steps Martin took: calibrate your mindset; engage your team to build, test and learn; and be the coach your people need.

Part 2. Mindset

The world of work has changed forever, and this part of the book begins with a corresponding call to action: *Be alert to the nature of challenges*.

What does that mean?

Not all workplace challenges are alike. Be aware of the differences between linear problems that have a known or logical solution versus the nonlinear, where it can be difficult even to define the problem let alone resolve it to the satisfaction of others.

Advantage leaders accept there are no perfect solutions in a nonlinear world, and that they will confront many tough decisions and trade-offs. Tanya Monro: 'We have had to pivot to the highest priorities, meaning hard, really hard decisions, but more importantly, really hard conversations about our role, what we do, what's important and what's no longer so important.'

Help your team to recognise nonlinear challenges and guide them to lean into the more difficult conversations about conflicting priorities and calls of judgement when there simply isn't data to fall back on.

Navigating high-demand nonlinear environments calls for an adaptive mindset. This approach is proactive and open to change, embracing new perspectives and opportunities for growth. It differs from a defensive mindset that resists or avoids challenges and potential risks.

The *Working model adaptive mindset* provides a quick reference guide to the characteristic ways of thinking and behaving with an adaptive mindset and its opposite.

Awareness of your own defensive mindset is an essential first step to succeeding in a high-demand environment because you are wired to respond defensively or protectively to threats. However, you can train your mindset to seek opportunity not security.

Three takeaways offer excellent foundations on which to build your toolkit:

» **Make adaptive mindset your foundation habit.** Adaptive mindset is the superpower on the pathway from adversity to advantage. Prioritise the habit of mindset awareness so you understand what triggers your defensiveness and why.

» **Embrace the squirm.** High-demand environments come with emotional squirm. Explore if you are held back by fear of uncertainty, of being exposed, or perhaps you steer away from conflict. Lean into the feelings; accept them as natural and expected. They are a sign you are on the right pathway.

» **Go towards the fire.** Those who excel under pressure tend to take a courageous and proactive approach to difficulties, instead of avoiding or denying them. Hold your power through difficulties, or as athletes say, 'hold your shape'.

Part 3. Recalibrate

Nothing highlights better the ability of turbulence to rapidly flip paradigms than the mass adoption of remote working during the pandemic. In just days, rules, principles, norms and habits went out the window right across the world.

Change in mindset and practices can and does happen at scale. And it's not just when we are confronted by a global pandemic. We saw it again in the exponential growth in generative AI following the release of ChatGPT, a disruption that has only just begun to fuel disruption in our lives and workplaces.

Advantage leaders see the disruption of paradigm shifts as two sided. On one side changes like the government policy flips in aged care and the increasing frequency and speed of industry-shaking incidents like the demise of Credit Suisse bank demand alertness and response. As VUCA prevails, 'business as usual' leaders will seek to understand the context and react accordingly. In contrast, advantage leaders will take the proactive option, to get ahead of the curve by challenging beliefs and assumptions to innovate ahead of disruption and in some cases be the cause of disruption. Proactive paradigm flips aren't limited to business models and technology. **humm**group did it by installing practices that have seen employee engagement scores go up not down during disruption. How? Rebecca James: 'We started during the pandemic with a company-wide get-together every single week, usually 15 minutes unless there's a bigger topic to explore. I would say it's been the single biggest input into an improvement in how engaged our team feel and our engagement score.'

Paradigms have shifted and continue to change, as a result. It's essential to recalibrate your mindset. Across four chapters we asked you to explore specific challenges, which address decision making, control, learning and wellbeing.

Four takeaways help you define your personal call to action.

> » **Anchor on personal values.** Surface and affirm your core values, so that when clarity and certainty are stripped away, you have a way to guide the decisions you make for yourself, your team and all those relying on your leadership.

» **Accept the externality of change.** Embrace uncertainty and ambiguity so you learn to lead with poise and certainty on the 'highway of uncertainty'.

» **Dial up the learning.** Apply the discipline of learning loops and strengthen your ability to source and process insights from the field.

» **Prioritise self-care.** Be alert to the costs of ignoring self-care, embed habits that suit your inner game, and place equal value on performance and wellbeing.

Part 4. Team up

How important is a high-performing team to your business aspirations?

Advantage leaders place it near the top and invest in people, tools and practices that build and connect teams.

That begins with the right people. Tanya Monro: 'A good team must have people who are really different. Otherwise, it's not a diverse, robust, resilient team.'

And the right fit. Brett Wickham: 'I can't overstate enough that you must recruit the right people and it's not the people with the right skills and experience. It's the people with the right fit.'

To build a high-performing team you need a shared understanding of the essential characteristics. The *Team Canvas* is your blueprint for team success. It describes and enables three team intentions: align, collaborate and learn.

Use the Team Canvas to evaluate your team, to envision the ways of working, then bring those to life using the tools for turbulence. You and your team will benefit from a shared language, the simplicity of the ACL loop and the power of an effective operating rhythm.

Align requires a commitment to a shared direction and focus. Make sure your team knows its purpose, has a compelling narrative to engage hearts and minds, commits to norms and standards of behaviour, and knows what must be delivered. Find or create shared tools like the *Team Diamond* and *Hearts and minds narrative* to help your team *align*. As Rebecca James notes, 'Team tools help navigate different disruptions like the changing macro environment. It means we can work in a much more agile way throughout the business and is key to leading through these times.'

Collaborate requires sharing in the spirit of working as one. Invest time and attention to connect your team through trust-based relationships so team members value one-to-one colleague partnerships as much as they value the collective team.

Shape your team's ways of working so everyone shares the big picture and shares the reality. Kate Koch: 'When our leaders collectively have a clear understanding of each team's achievements it opens up the conversations about the elephants in the room.'

Leverage the benefits of collaborating openly around problems, opportunities and decisions, taking confidence from Paul Duldig's observation, 'People make incredibly sensible decisions when they have the right kind of conversations.'

Learn requires your team to adapt at pace and on the run. Prioritise team awareness by being open to reflection, to seek, give and receive feedback and to challenge. Chris Tanti: 'Make sure that you're dialling into what is really going on rather than what you'd like to be going on.'

Build an operating rhythm that will ensure your tempo prevails when the storms arrive. Embed action debriefing so your team gets better at delivering outcomes at pace while continuing to learn and adapt. Paul Ostrowski: 'The 90-day operating rhythm has given us adaptability in an ambiguous environment, and it has also promoted communication, support, accountability and confidence amongst the team.'

Four takeaways are your call to action to build a high-performing team.

» **Define your team blueprint.** Complete the evaluation exercise on the Team Canvas and then use the insights to shape your ACL.

» **Align for total commitment**. Be relentless in checking that your team is aligned. If you don't give this constant attention, the only sure thing in turbulence is misalignment.

» **Collaborate as one**. Introduce the 'five shares' to your team and talk about their hopes and concerns in each of the shares. Explore ways to build a *one team culture* because that makes anything possible.

» **Make team learning a habit**. Pay attention to your operating rhythm because in changeable conditions the ACL depends more on *Learn* than it does on *Align* or *Collaborate*. Why? Because a team that learns can realign and improve collaboration no matter their situation.

Part 5. Coach

The call to action here is to 'be the coach your people need'.

What do they need?

Each member of your team is an individual and they will each react differently as they face into emotion-charged environments. They might feel stretched beyond their limits, or isolated and buffeted by unexpected and unwanted change. Alternatively, they could see possibilities and want to explore new directions. They need a leader with empathy for their situation, with the skills and tools to at times support them and at other times challenge them.

Successful coaches prioritise relationships over more traditional leadership practices. Remember Ashley Ross's observation: 'It's about the people being coached having real trust that the coach is there for them and that they do care.'

To adopt the role of coach you must adjust your thinking to put people first and prioritise their wellbeing, needs and growth above all else. It may mean changing the way you act, as Kate Koch remarked earlier: 'Being a distant leader is a thing of the past.'

A constant across advantage leaders is their willingness to be more open and vulnerable while retaining poise and confidence.

Sally Capp observes, 'Taking risks on people and their own decision making is critical and means being more open, and potentially more vulnerable. Being more willing to show that you don't have all the answers, but maintain the ability to demonstrate leadership in action.'

Be the coach who looks for the potential in people, in their team and in their enterprise. Cultivate the mindset and tools of a coach and you will unlock potential by providing people with the support, guidance and challenge they need to be the best they can be.

Three takeaways define your call to action to be the coach.

» **Put people first.** Reflect on your natural 'go to' approach. Is it people first, second or last? Would you be a more effective leader if you embraced one or more people-first behaviours?

» **Make vulnerability a strength.** Be ready to openly and authentically share personal emotions and experiences with others. Look for opportunities to admit your uncertainty, ask for help and take thoughtful risks.

» **Go one to one.** Ramp up your one-on-one conversations with your team and engage them in ADEP conversations. Make performance partnering a habit and leadership trademark.

Part 6. Scale

We hope this book has inspired you to strengthen your leadership at a personal, team and enterprise level. If it has, then the change you want will inevitably start with you and your habits. And it won't be linear.

You may choose to start with just one tool, perhaps Adaptive Mindset or ADEP, and apply that today in your work, in your life, with your team, or across the team of teams that comprises your enterprise. On the other hand, you may choose to go deep and far, adopting many of the tools and practices we've outlined. It's your choice, there's no perfect answer because it's adaptive and you will loop and learn as you balance dealing with the short-term imperatives and the longer-term strategic decisions.

Bernadette McDonald advises, 'Find that balance of strategic vision, future thinking with being very deliberate in asking, "What are we doing every day and how do we keep the performance going and get better".'

To help with that choice reflect on questions in three domains — *self, team* and *enterprise.*

» **Self — at work and in life.** There are important boundaries between work and the rest of your life, however many of the practices of advantage leaders are whole-of-life habits. For example, adaptive mindset is as valuable in parenting as in coaching, and self-care can't be compartmentalised and still effective. Paul Duldig: 'Self-care is essential and you need a number of different outlets over time to recharge the batteries.' Here are three prompts we recommend as life habits to help build and sustain your toolkit for turbulence:

■ **Prioritise self-reflection:** Take regular time for self-reflection to assess your own performance and wellbeing, and to look for strengths and areas to improve.

■ **Do your own ADEP:** Use the ADEP framework to set and evaluate your goals and priorities. Review every 90 days to maintain a suitable balance of achievement, development, enjoyment and partnering.

- **Practise self-care:** Implement self-care practices such as exercise, mindfulness and adequate rest to enhance your overall wellbeing and resilience.

» **Team — as individuals and collectively.** The *Team Canvas* is your 'go to' framework to assess strengths and gaps, and to set aspirations and ways of working. Follow Brett Wickham's guidance: 'Trust your team more, especially as the business grows. Give them accountability and responsibility and measure their success with genuine feedback.' To create the optimal team ACL setup and operating rhythm here are three prompts to help build and sustain your toolkit:

- **Foster open communication:** The greatest advantage you can give your team is to foster a safe space for open dialogue, problem solving and idea sharing.

- **Make it personal:** The one-to-one relationship is vital, and many tools like performance partnering will help you to build and strengthen these essential connections.

- **Enable continuous feedback:** The lifeblood of team adaptability is the loop of alignment, collaboration and learning, so be attentive to the operating rhythm and the discipline of reflection and debriefing.

» **Enterprise — leaders and team of teams.** The tools covered in this book are tested and proven to help build unity among leadership cohorts and to strengthen team-to-team collaboration. Use them to seize the opportunity to scale your own leadership influence and positive impact. Recognise your responsibility to fill the vacuums across the enterprise. Robert Iervasi: 'Don't allow stakeholders, whether employees, suppliers or customers, to operate by perception. Be open, articulate, transparent. Silence is one of the greatest barriers that you can have in an organisation.' Here are three prompts to scale your toolkit and impact.

- **Share your knowledge:** Share your experiences and lessons learned from applying the leadership toolkit in cross-enterprise meetings, inspiring others to embrace and leverage the new tools.

- **Facilitate cross-team collaboration:** Sponsor cross-functional meetings or projects to encourage collaboration and sharing between different departments or teams.

- **Build strategic partnerships:** Use the partnering tools to seek opportunities to build partnerships with key stakeholders across the organisation and wider ecosystem to foster collaboration and shared goals.

Yes, there is a lot to consider, but this is your moment and you need a big toolkit.

Hear Tanya Monro's call to action: 'When it's turbulent and when it's tough, that is the opportunity for leaders to make impact and shine. When things are smooth you're really window dressing!'

It's time to make your choices, so here is a snapshot of the primary tools and where you can find them in the book.

Primary tools

Primary tools are your 'go to' resources to master key challenges and unlock potential. They are supported by secondary tools that add to your resources to move from adversity to advantage. To help you implement the tools, canvases provide a visual template to organise thoughts and map action plans.

THE PATHWAY (PAGE 8)

The three phases of the pathway — *disruption, adaptability, advantage* — capture the essence of the advantage leader's approach. Use it as a mental model and a conversation starter with your team and colleagues to find creative opportunities in disruption and to strengthen adaptive capabilities.

RECOGNISE LINEAR AND NONLINEAR PROBLEMS (PAGE 35)

Most significant leadership challenges have nonlinear elements such as a hard-to-define problem, unclear or unknown solutions, or emotion-charged and conflicting views. Use this tool to build your own awareness of the differences between linear and nonlinear problems and to consider the leadership implications.

TEAM TALK. BE ALERT TO THE NONLINEAR (PAGE 41)

A team that recognises, understands and effectively navigates nonlinear problems can minimise the risks of resistance to change, mistrust and politics that derail strategies and plans. This tool guides you to facilitate your team to see the vital distinction between linear and nonlinear challenges and to apply the right mindset and skills to the right problems.

WORKING MODEL ADAPTIVE MINDSET (PAGE 48)

This tool uses the Adaptive Mindset model as a quick reference guide to the characteristic ways of thinking and behaving with an adaptive mindset and its opposite, a defensive mindset. Many advantage leaders keep a copy of the model near their workstation to prompt awareness and reflection of this foundation concept.

MINDSET AWARENESS TRAINING (PAGE 50)

Mindset awareness training is designed to raise awareness of your protective and defensive responses to threats, and to reorient towards an adaptive mindset. The *Mindset Training Canvas* provides a map to guide you through the three steps in mindset awareness training — *See, Squirm, Seek*. The canvas is also used in facilitated workshops to debrief tough situations and capture insights and learning.

ANCHOR ON PERSONAL VALUES (PAGE 91)

Personal values are the foundation on which to make tough choices and decisions. This tool guides you to identify your core values, place them in a values frame, use them as a foundation for decision making, and decide whether you are ready to share the frame and story with your team.

CROSS THE HIGHWAY OF UNCERTAINTY (PAGE 102)

Uncertainty is a common and recurring characteristic of the business landscape. This tool challenges you to reflect on your relationship with uncertainty and ambiguity, and provides a mental model to build confidence to engage with and lead through uncertainty.

SELF-CARE PLAN (PAGE 143)

Ongoing workplace turbulence compels advantage leaders to pay attention to performance and wellbeing. This tool employs the *Self-care Canvas* to guide your thought process to understand the triggers to three mind zones, then to plan and commit to effective and sustainable self-care habits to support your wellbeing.

TEAM CANVAS (PAGE 160)

The *Team Canvas* provides the blueprint to evaluate your team setup. The one-page map is a great way to step through the key building blocks of high-performance teamwork.

BEAUTIFUL PARADOXES (PAGE 174)

Turbulence is chock full of paradoxes, and teams do better when these are surfaced and talked about. This tool does exactly that by guiding you to facilitate a team activity. This is a handy exercise in team building and strategic and business planning, and can be incorporated into leadership development activities.

CO-CREATING THE TEAM PURPOSE (PAGE 177)

Despite what most teams report, it is rare to find a team in which all the members can articulate a clear and common team purpose. That's where a simple, powerful set of five questions can help your team to clarify purpose, lift beyond what they do, and see a higher purpose that is all about transformation. Use this tool in concert with the next tool, *Team Diamond*.

TEAM DIAMOND (PAGE 180)

This simple 'go-to' tool has proven itself time and again to effectively achieve team alignment, particularly in leadership teams where a siloed approach prevails. The *Team Diamond* itself is a simple model that you can use to cut through complexity and connect purpose and priorities. The end product provides an excellent framework to guide meeting agendas and partnering between team members.

HEARTS AND MINDS NARRATIVE (PAGE 183)

How do you build passion and cohesion around a shared vision, and capture the hearts and minds of people who are important to its achievement? That's where this tool and the accompanying *Narrative Canvas* provide a step-by-step guide to creating a compelling narrative of your team's vision. Dive in and have some fun with villains, the quest and a call to action.

TEAM COMMITMENTS (BEHAVIOURS) (PAGE 189)

Most high-performing teams have an explicit or implicit commitment to standards of team behaviour. This tool provides a straightforward process, including an example, to help your team to define or hone their commitments to each other. This process relies on a psychologically safe environment so people are open in discussing, defining then holding on to those standards.

90-DAY TEAM DELIVERABLES (PAGE 196)

This is your facilitation guide to define the most important outcomes for your team to deliver over the next performance cycle. This helps with alignment and is an efficient way to achieve clarity and agreement; 90 days is the recommended default cycle and the *Deliverables Canvas* supports the activity by giving team members a shared framework to define key outcomes.

FIVE SHARES (ABOVE THE LINE / BELOW THE LINE) (PAGE 208)

The Think One Team Five Shares model provides a framework to help your team to see what working as one team means in simple practical behaviours. Use this as a conversation starter about collaboration, and as an engaging and effective way to identify opportunities to leverage team strengths and address potential derailers.

I-CORE TRUST MODEL (PAGE 213)

This tool uses the I-CORE model as the starting point for building trust-based relationships between colleagues, within and between teams, and for strategic partnering. The items — *integrity, competence, openness, reliability, equity* — offer an excellent and pragmatic guide to weigh up and choose the optimal way to strengthen important relationships and connections.

PARTNERING QUADRANT IN ACTION (PAGE 226)

The *Partnering Quadrant in action* describes the four essential steps to building and sustaining partnering relationships. Each quadrant refers to a conversation, which in turn helps to establish rapport, expectations, agreements and ongoing partnering. This provides a practical guide to partnering between teams and with colleagues and stakeholders.

PROBED COLLABORATIVE PROBLEM SOLVER (PAGE 231)

The capabilities and practices of collaborative problem solving are among the most important contributors to team agility and effectiveness. This tool is engagingly simple and works on the principle that a shared tool for problem solving is a disarmingly effective way to get people to work together across boundaries. The *PROBED Canvas* describes a six-step process.

THREE POINTS INSIGHTS (PAGE 253)

Few practices strengthen a team more effectively than well-designed conversations in which members seek insights and feedback from colleagues. This tool introduces a process that allows the leader to role model openness to insights and as a result sets the tone for others to follow.

ACTION DEBRIEF (PAGE 257)

There are countless ways to structure a team debrief, and varying the approach helps to keep a freshness to the conversations. This tool introduces a step-by-step guide to the most basic of debrief processes, and includes suggestions to facilitate openness to learn and improve.

OPERATING RHYTHM REVIEW (PAGE 264)

The ideal operating rhythm works for you, your team and stakeholders. This tool provides a process, guided by the *Operating Rhythm Canvas*, to evaluate and find your optimal operating rhythm. The process includes defining current and desired rituals, operating principles, and key events and activities.

SEVEN SIGNS OF VULNERABILITY (PAGE 288)

Vulnerability is all about your readiness to openly and authentically share personal experiences and emotions with others. For leaders the ability to be vulnerable can be powerful, which is why this tool, guided by the *Seven signs of vulnerability* model, has proven to be very useful to help leaders build more open and trusting relationships with their team and colleagues.

UNDERSTAND THE ADEP MODEL (PAGE 294)

The ADEP model and accompanying *ADEP 90-day Canvas* is your guide to four essential aspects of sustainable performance. It provides a mental model and guide for your coaching of individual team members and is used in the *Performance partnering* tool to reimagine the role and nature of performance conversations.

PERFORMANCE PARTNERING (PAGE 300)

The traditional performance management process is ill-equipped for turbulent times. A more agile and practical process is needed to enable more frequent and balanced performance conversations. The *Performance Partnering Canvas* guides this process and offers a practical and proven way to help leaders and team members to sustain performance and wellbeing.

Choose wisely

In this book we have covered an extraordinary range of concepts and tools. It's now up to you to decide which of them to add to your toolkit and over time how you will use them and shape them to extract maximum value for yourself, your team and your enterprise. Be sure to visit www.toolkitforturbulence.com for supplemental support materials and updates we've designed to help you build and refresh your toolkit.

We suggest you start by plotting a direction of travel, your north star, then choose one or two tools to get started. It doesn't matter whether your first move is to lightly tweak your attitude from defensive to adaptive in the face of a challenge, to add a personal habit for self-care to fuel your energy, or to bring your team together and recast their purpose and operating rhythm. Remember, there are no right answers that work for everyone. There are just best answers for your context and leadership journey. As Kevin Sullivan reminded us with his heroic leadership, we must first keep the plane flying then deal with other things.

New habits in self-care will put wind beneath your wings, as will relationships built on care, trust and generosity. Tough calls need to be made. Turbulence is not comfortable, but it can be exciting, inspiring and rewarding provided you look beyond the potential for disaster and instead see the opportunity for advantage.

All the best

Graham Winter and Martin Bean

Acknowledgements

Together we want to thank those who helped, guided and supported us in creating this book and the accompanying resources.

Kylie Smith, thank you for your tireless care, coordination and attention to every detail needed to bring this to life for us as the authors, for our co-creators and the whole business community. Your efforts have been outstanding and we are forever grateful.

To our wonderful co-creators who are named in the opening section of the book. Your openness and generosity in sharing your very personal experience of turbulence is the golden thread that holds this book together.

To Brett Penno for helping us to create the simple and engaging website to connect the book to the tools that leaders and teams need to create their own toolkits.

To Kristine Chompff for supporting our launch and marketing efforts.

To Lucy Raymond, Leigh McLennon, Chris Shorten, Renee Aurish, Jem Bates and the whole Wiley Team for seeing the potential in this book, and for the speed and agility in creating such a great looking product.

To Justina Ko from e-blossomly for your creativity and partnering to cocreate the video trailer that so powerfully tells the story of *Toolkit for Turbulence*.

To Scott Eathorne, thank you for committing to help us publicise the important messages in the book to the wider world.

FROM GRAHAM WINTER

Thank you to Carol for your love and for yet again encouraging me to pursue my dreams. To Mark, Ben and your families thank you for giving so much love and joy to Carol and myself. Thank you to Gill Duck and Mark Williams for your ideas, support and guidance along the way, and to Ron Steiner for always being my go-to person for feedback and perspective. To the many mentors and guides who shaped my life and career including but not limited to my parents Muriel and Bill Winter, my sister Helen Winter, Chester Bennett, Reg Davis, Dr Adrian Porter, and of course my co-author Martin Bean.

To the almost countless clients, colleagues, partners and support team who have enabled me to pursue a fulfilling career, you have given me so much in treasured memories and relationships.

FROM MARTIN BEAN

To my wife, Mary – your love, care, and support have been the driving force behind this new chapter in my life and career. To our amazing daughters, Maddie, Georgie and Harriet, thank you for your belief, love and friendship. To my incredible Vice Chancellor's Executive, who made the impossible possible and overcame all obstacles together. Helen Souness for your encouragement to capture my wisdom and experiences in this VUCA world. To my amazing co-author, Graham – your unwavering friendship and support anchored me during the most demanding leadership experience. Your insights and determination made this book possible. To my parents, Margaret, Alf, Marion, and Jim, for instilling in me the values of courage, care and mateship that shaped who I am today.

To all those whose names may not appear on these pages but have contributed in their own way – thank you. Your support, encouragement, and presence have been instrumental in making this book a reality.

References

Chapter 1

Taleb, N. N. (2013). *Antifragile*. Penguin.

Bennis, W., and Nanus, B. (1985). *Leaders: The strategies for taking charge*. Harper & Row.

'In-flight upset — Airbus A330-303, VH-QPA, 154 km west of Learmonth, WA, 7 October 2008'. Australian Transport Safety Bureau.

Sullivan, K. (2019). *No man's land*. HarperCollins.

Prochnau, W., and Parker, L. (2009). *Miracle on the Hudson: The survivors of flight 1549 tell their extraordinary stories of courage, faith, and determination*. Ballantine Books.

Chapter 2

Smith, D. (2022). 'Stolen NZ data listed for sale on dark web', *Stuff*. https://www.stuff.co.nz/business/130813253/stolen-nz-data-listed-for-sale-on-dark-web (accessed: 10 May 2023).

'Aviate – Navigate – Communicate'. Flight Standards Service (2001). Instrument flying handbook. US Dept of Transportation, Federal Aviation Administration.

Kuhn, T. S. (1962). *The structure of scientific revolutions*. University of Chicago Press.

Chapter 3

Heifetz, R. (2009). *The practice of adaptive leadership: Tools and tactics for changing your organization and the world*. Harvard Kennedy School.

Heifetz, R. (1998). *Leadership without easy answers*. Harvard University Press.

Chapter 4

Organizational Culture Change and Leadership, Human Synergistics, https://www.humansynergistics.com/

Maslow, A.H. (1943). '*A Theory of Human Motivation*'. *Psychological Review*, 50(4), 430–437.

Rock, D. (2009). 'SCARF: a brain-based model for collaborating with and influencing others', *Semantic Scholar*.

Chapter 5

Dobbs, M. (2009). *One minute to midnight: Kennedy, Khrushchev, and Castro on the brink of nuclear war*. Vintage.

Barker, J. A. (1989). *Discovering the future: The business of paradigms*. HarperBusiness.

Chapter 6

Taleb, N. N. (2012). *The black swan: The impact of the highly improbable*. Penguin.

Chapter 7

Overmier, J. B., and Seligman, M. E. (1967). 'Effects of inescapable shock upon subsequent escape and avoidance responding', *Journal of Comparative Physiological Psychology* 63(1), 28–33.

Seligman, M. E. P. (2018). *Learned optimism: How to change your mind and your life*. Nicholas Brealey Publishing.

Collins, J. (2011). *Good to great: Why some companies make the leap . . . and others don't*. HarperBusiness.

Stockdale Paradox, 'hopeful optimism' and 'helpless pessimism'. See Collins.

Harding, M. (2018). *3 ways to get comfortable with ambiguity*, IDEO. https://www.ideo.com/blog/3-ways-to-get-comfortable-with-ambiguity?hss_channel=lcp-164291 (accessed: 11 May 2023).

Kübler-Ross, E. (1973). *On death and dying*. Macmillan.

Bridges, W., Bridges, S. M., and Lin, X. (2020). *Transitions: Making sense of life's changes*. Da Capo Books.